Roly Smith

111 Places in the Peak District That You Shouldn't Miss

Photographs by Chris Gilbert

emons:

Cäcilienstraße 48, 50667 Köln
info@emons-verlag.de

Layout: Eva Kraskes, based on a design
by Lübbeke | Naumann | Thoben
Maps: altancicek.design, www.altancicek.de
Basic cartographical information from Openstreetmap,
© OpenStreetMap-Mitwirkende, OdbL
Edited by: Tania Taylor
Printing and binding: sourc-e GmbH
Printed in Europe 2026
ISBN 978-3-7408-2551-5
First edition

Guidebooks for Locals & Experienced Travellers
Join us in uncovering new places around the world at
www.111places.com

Foreword

If you look at a satellite photograph of the British Isles taken on a clear night, all you can see are the street lights of urban settlements. And you'll note that there's an obvious, boxing glove-shaped island of darkness right in the middle of England, sandwiched between the glowing street lights of Greater Manchester, Sheffield, the West Midlands and West Yorkshire.

That island of blackness is the sparsely populated Peak District National Park, the first to be designated in Britain and – at 555 square miles – a miraculous survival of beautiful limestone dales and bleak gritstone moorland, right on the doorsteps of most of the teeming populations of largely industrial northern England.

There are two sharply contrasting faces of the Peak District, which some people have given male and female characteristics. The White Peak (feminine) is the name given to the oldest rocks of the Peak, the Carboniferous limestone formed around 350 million years ago. These give rise to the 1,000-foot-high central and southern plateau of the Peak, which is threaded by glorious dales such as Dovedale, Lathkill Dale and Monsal Dale.

In sharp contrast – and enclosing this to the north, west and east – is the Dark Peak (masculine), which takes its name from the darker, higher rocks of Millstone Grit and shale. These are characterised by bleak, barren moorlands and vertical escarpments – here known as 'edges' – where the moors step steeply down to rivers such as the Derwent and the Wye.

But there are many unmissable places in both the White and Dark Peaks, such as those described in this book under their respective geological divisions, which you should include in your itinerary. Also included are some of the surrounding towns, such as Buxton and Matlock Bath, which are usually included in what is known as the greater Peak District.

111 Places

Walks

1 Bakewell Bridge

The bridges of Bakewell

It's an extraordinary fact, but Bakewell's famous and much-photographed five-arch bridge over the River Wye has been carrying traffic for over 700 years. It is claimed to be the oldest still 'working' bridge in England.

The earliest record for a stone bridge here is 1272, but the present structure was built in the early 14th century. Due to increased traffic on the main Bakewell to Chesterfield road, the bridge was substantially but sympathetically widened on the north side in the 19th century to give it a width of 23 feet. The total span is 120 feet.

Constructed of weathered ashlar sandstone, each slightly pointed arch has a span of 20 feet, resting on triangular cutwaters that rise to form pedestrian refuges in the bridge above. During the Covid epidemic, the narrow, paved footpath on either side was converted to one-way traffic.

Just downstream from Bakewell Bridge is the Weir Bridge, which was constructed as part of the Bakewell Town Centre redevelopment in the 1980s as a link between the main car parks and the town centre. This stylish single-arch bridge became very popular with visitors, who adorned the supporting wires with an estimated 40,000 'love locks' – padlocks with messages expressing their feelings for loved ones.

But the weight of the locks was threatening the structure of the bridge, and as part of a refurbishment of the entire structure, Derbyshire County Council had them removed in 2024. There was a huge public outcry at this, and eventually, the love locks were reinstalled at nearby Thornbridge Hall.

Upstream from Bakewell Bridge is Holme Bridge, a five-arched packhorse bridge first mentioned in 1562. The narrow, four-foot-wide present bridge was built in 1664 and is protected as an Ancient Monument. Close by is a sheepfold where the animals were kept before their cleansing dip in the river.

Address Bridge Street, Bakewell, DE45 1DS | Getting there On the A617 Bakewell to Chesterfield road | Hours Accessible 24 hours | Tip Bakewell's Old House Museum in Cunningham Place, Bakewell (+44 (0) 1629 813642), originally built by Joseph Arkwright, is a treasure house of artefacts and exhibits illustrating the history of the town.

2 Bakewell Puddings

The proof of the pudding

Mention the name of Bakewell to most people and they will immediately think of the sickly-sweet dessert universally known as the Bakewell Pudding – which incidentally bears no resemblance to Mr Kipling's icing-covered tart topped with a cherry. The origins of the famous pudding, a delicacy now known all round the world, are, to use that time-honoured phrase, lost in the mists of time. No one really knows who invented it but they all seem to agree that it happened in the kitchen of The Rutland Arms Hotel in the Market Square of Bakewell, sometime in the early 19th century.

A commonly held but unsubstantiated belief is that one day when important visitors were expected for dinner, Mrs Ann Greaves, the respected innkeeper for over 40 years, instructed her cook to make a strawberry tart, stirring the egg mixture into the pastry with the jam on top. The cook, whose name is unfortunately lost to history, mistakenly poured the egg and sugar mixture *over* the jam, so what was supposed to be a tart became a pudding. Quite unexpectedly, the resultant purely accidental dessert became a great hit with Mrs Greaves' guests and it has been made that way ever since.

The modern Bakewell Pudding is a very rich, almond-flavoured pudding with a flaky pastry base and a jam-filled centre. But always serve your Bakewell Pudding hot – the taste is just not the same when it's served cold.

Several bakeries and shops in the town now make and serve the pudding, including the flower-bedecked and much-photographed, Grade II-listed, 18th-century Old Original Bakewell Pudding Shop in The Square, originally owned by the Wilson family, who claimed to have obtained the secret recipe directly from Mrs Greaves up the road. It's one of at least two shops in Bakewell that claim to hold the original recipe for the Bakewell Pudding, which is now securely locked away in their safe, so the secret remains inviolate.

Address The Old Original Bakewell Pudding Shop, The Square, Bakewell, DE45 1BT, +44 (0) 1629 812193 | Getting there Bakewell is on the A6 between Matlock and Buxton | Hours Shop: Mon–Sat 8.30am–6pm, Sun 9am–6pm; restaurant daily 9am–5pm | Tip The restaurant on the first floor of the Old Original Bakewell Pudding Shop claims to have been serving Bakewell Puddings since 1860, so tuck in and enjoy a Bakewell there or in one of the other restaurants in town.

3 Bakewell Saxon Crosses

Thousand-year-old works of art

There are nearly 40 pieces of Anglo-Saxon and Anglo-Scandinavian sculpture in and around the hilltop parish church of All Saints, Bakewell, making it one of the biggest collections of stonework from this period in the country.

With the other Anglian churchyard crosses found at Eyam, Hope, Bradbourne and Ilam, it has been suggested that Bakewell may have been the centre for the makers of these intricately carved monuments, some of which may date from as early as the 8th century.

Prominent among Bakewell's outstanding collection are two crosses, which once stood out in the countryside as wayside preaching crosses, but which have been incorporated into the churchyard. These 1,000-year-old works of art are both now badly eroded, having been subject to a millennium of Peak District weather.

The largest cross, which now stands enclosed behind railings by the east end of the church, is a fine if truncated example, profusely decorated with figures, animals, vine scrolling and a crucifixion scene. The second smaller cross outside the south porch is headless but covered in intricate interlacing knotwork. It originally stood at Two Dales, near Darley Dale.

Inside the church, hands raised in prayer and looking out as if from a crocketed window, Sir Godfrey de Foljambe (1317–1376) and his wife, Avena (1320–1382), gaze stonily from their monument in the chancel as they have for six centuries. The mural alabaster monument to the waist-high couple, installed in 1385, is very rare, with only two other similar examples surviving today.

Foljambe was born at Tideswell in 1317, the fourth son of Sir Thomas de Foljambe and Alice Foljambe. The family were Lords of the Manor of Tideswell with lands at Darley Dale. Godfrey succeeded to the family estates after the death of his three elder brothers, when he also acquired the manor of Bakewell.

Address All Saints Parish Church, South Church Street, Bakewell, DE45 1FD | **Getting there** Off the A6 between Matlock and Buxton | **Hours** Accessible 24 hours | **Tip** Come to Bakewell on a Monday and you can enjoy one of the best street markets in the county, in the Market Square behind the Old Market Hall.

4 The Barrel Inn

A pub with a view

If you are looking for a pub with a view, then The Barrel Inn at Bretton will take some beating. Standing at a lofty 1,250 feet above sea level, The Barrel is the highest pub in Derbyshire, with the views from its front door allegedly extending over five counties. It certainly extends southwards over much of the rolling White Peak plateau, as far as the tree-topped Neolithic chambered tomb of Minninglow on the High Peak Trail some 15 miles away.

The Times newspaper also recently named The Barrel as one of the cosiest pubs in the country. With its nail-studded doors, stone-flagged floor, oak beams and thick limestone walls strung with gleaming brasses and usually a welcoming log fire as you enter, it's hard to argue with that assessment by 'The Thunderer'.

Built in 1597 originally with a heather-thatched roof, The Barrel Inn is situated at the head of Bretton Clough on a commandingly high ridge between the villages of Eyam and Great Hucklow. It is thought that the original inn may have been at nearby Nether Bretton Farm, and the first recorded landlord was George Bowman, who served behind the bar until 1770.

Over the years The Barrel has served as a kind of roadside watering hole of its time. Bretton Moor was crossed by an ancient bridleway from Hathersage to Eyam, which met up with the main Sheffield, Dronfield and Chesterfield bridleways. In medieval times the route was used for transporting supplies of salt from Cheshire to the burgeoning township of Sheffield and points east. The 1757 turnpike road linking Sheffield, Ringinglow, Longshaw, Great Hucklow, Tideswell, Wormhill and Buxton also went past the inn.

Providing further excitement and interest for visitors is that due to its lofty elevation, The Barrel is now also a favourite launch site for gliders and hang gliders, which soar effortlessly in the thermals created by the ridge on which it stands.

Address The Barrel Inn, Bretton, Hope Valley, S32 5QD, +44 (0) 1433 630856 | Getting there The Barrel Inn is on the minor road between Eyam and Great Hucklow | Hours Bar: daily all day; Restaurant: Mon–Sat noon–2pm & 6–8pm, Sun noon–5pm | Tip A little further along the minor road that leads to The Barrel, at Camphill Farm on Hucklow Edge, is the Derbyshire & Lancashire Gliding Club (+44 (0) 1298 871270). The club has been operating from its spectacular site since 1936 and offers exhilarating glider flight experiences over the Peak District for visitors.

5 Black Rocks

Birthplace of rock climbing

Black Rocks is an impressive, tree-topped outcrop of Ashover gritstone between Cromford and Wirksworth that occupies an important place in the history of British rock climbing.

Some of the earliest rock climbs in the Peak District were accomplished at Black Rocks, including seminal climbs by pioneers such as J. W. Puttrell, Fred Pigott and Peter Harding. The crag has been a well-known climbing venue since the 1890s, and features in the 1913 guidebook *Some Gritstone Climbs.*

It is most noted in the climbing world today for its extreme climbing routes put up in the mid 1980s to the early 2000s by ace free climbers like Johnny Dawes. But Black Rocks has some 100 traditional climbing routes of grades ranging from 'Difficult' to 'Very Severe', and a selection of short bouldering problems. Most extreme is the 'terrifying' 65-foot Gaia, which follows the steep shallow groove in the front face of the rocks.

The area around the Black Rocks site was anciently mined for lead, and the spoil left behind on the scree slope leading up to the rocks supports many lead-tolerant plants such as leadwort (spring sandwort) and mountain pansy.

Black Rocks is the centrepiece of a Derbyshire County Council country park, and the five-minute climb up onto the graffiti-scarred top of the gritstone outcrop is rewarded with superb views across the Matlock Gorge towards Riber Castle and the Derwent Mills World Heritage Site. Waymarked walks will also guide you through the Forestry Commission woodlands and heather of Cromford Moor, and you can access other beautiful countryside, including the mercifully traffic-free High Peak Trail, formerly the Cromford and High Peak Railway, which runs through the trees beneath the Black Rocks. The High Peak Trail runs for 17 miles between Cromford and Dowlow.

Address Black Rocks car park, near Cromford, DE4 4GT | Getting there Signposted off the B5036 between Cromford and Wirksworth | Hours Accessible 24 hours | Tip Scarthin Books, overlooking the village pond on The Promenade at Cromford (+44 (0) 1629 823272), is a treasure house for the bookworm, and has a vegetarian café with indoor and outdoor seating.

6 Boot's Folly

Fantastic folly is a false castle

Often mistakenly identified as a ruined castle, a notable landmark on the scenic Strines Road between the A57 and Langsett is the four-square, crenellated Boot's Folly, standing as a lone sentinel on the southern flanks of the Strines Reservoir.

But it was constructed as recently as 1927 by Charles Boot, son of the founder of local building company Henry Boot, who lived at nearby Sugworth Hall. The 45-foot-high, 20-foot-square tower, also sometimes known as Strines Tower or Sugworth Tower, stands in grand isolation at a height of 1,033 feet above the sea.

It is believed that the folly was constructed by Boot to provide work for his Sugworth Hall builders during the Great Depression. Another theory is that he built the tower so he could see High Bradfield churchyard where his wife, Bertha, who had died aged 56 in 1926, was buried.

In a commendable example of recycling, the folly was built from stone left over from the construction of nearby Bents House, which in turn had used stone from the disused Bents Farm, Pears House Farm and Nether Holes Farm. The three farms were demolished when the Strines Reservoir was built in 1869 because it was feared they would pollute the waters feeding the reservoir.

The Strines Reservoir was one of four built in Bradfield Dale by the Sheffield Water Committee in the late 19th century to provide drinking water for Sheffield. The reservoir has a grassy dam wall about 1,083 feet in length and 95 feet high, which floods an area of 54 acres, and holds 452,900,000 gallons of water.

Today the interior of the folly is bare. It originally had wood panelling and a large furnished room at the top, where the Boot family could enjoy the view down Bradfield Dale. There was a spiral staircase to the top, but this was removed some years ago after a cow climbed the stairs and became stuck.

Address Strines Reservoir, Bradfield, Sheffield, S6 6JA | Getting there A short, uphill walk from the dam of the Strines Reservoir | Hours Accessible 24 hours | Tip Overlooking the Strines Reservoir is The Strines Inn, (+44 (0) 1142 851247), one of the oldest pubs in the Peak District. Originally a 13th-century manor house, it was converted to an inn in 1771.

7 Bradfield Watch House

Foiling the body-snatchers

During the 19th century, a profitable trade could be made by so-called 'resurrectionists', who excavated the graves of newly interred bodies and sold them to medical schools for the study of anatomy. Probably the best known of these grave robbers were the infamous Burke and Hare, who plied their grisly trade in Edinburgh.

In 1831, the hilltop village of High Bradfield decided to try to put a stop to this illicit activity by building a Watch House (now a private house) at the entrance to the churchyard of St Nicholas. This would allow a guard to watch over the graveyard and apprehend potential grave robbers. It is one of very few buildings of this type that still exist in Britain.

At the time, stealing a corpse was punishable by a fine or imprisonment rather than transportation or execution, so body snatchers found it sufficiently profitable to run the risk. Ironically, the Anatomy Act passed in the next year (1832) ended the trade by allowing bodies to be donated to medical schools.

The Grade I-listed St Nicholas church itself is well worth a visit, occupying one of the most commanding views of any in the Peak District. Overlooking the Agden Reservoir, it extends far to the west over the heather-clad Bradfield and Broomhead Moors towards the distant Margery Hill.

Formerly the scene of well-attended classical music festivals, St Nicholas dates from the 12th century, and the interior boasts a Saxon Cross, a Norman font and 17 beautiful stained glass windows dating from the late 19th century.

Hidden by trees just behind the church is Bailey Hill, described as 'one of the best preserved and most dramatic motte-and-baileys (castles) in Yorkshire'. Motte and baileys were the earliest form of Norman castles and this is one of two 'castle' sites in the village. Castle Hill to the south of the village is thought to have been a Saxon ringwork.

Address The Watch House, Jane Lane, High Bradfield, S6S6 6LG | Getting there Off the B6077, about six miles west of Sheffield | Hours Viewable from the outside only | Tip High Bradfield has a great pub – The Old Horns Inn in Towngate (+44 (0) 1142 851207) – which has arguably one of the best views from any beer garden in the Peak District.

8 The Cage

Scene of Mr Darcy's famous dip

Instantly recognisable as Pemberley, home of Mr Darcy (played by Colin Firth) and scene of his celebrated dip in the lake in the 1995 BBC1 adaptation of Jane Austen's novel *Pride and Prejudice*, Lyme Park is a stately Palladian mansion on the western edge of the Peak District near Disley.

Home to the Legh family for over six centuries, Lyme Park remained in their possession until 1946, when it was passed to the National Trust. The estate had been granted to Sir Thomas d'Anyers in 1346 and passed by marriage to the Legh family in 1388.

The most obvious feature in the 1,359-acre deer park that surrounds the house is the tower known as The Cage, which stands on a prominent hill to the north of the house. It was originally a hunting lodge and a park-keeper's cottage, and was later used as a lock-up for prisoners, which is probably how it gained its name.

The first building was erected about 1580 as a hunting lodge for the Legh family, much like the Hunting Tower for the Cavendishes at Chatsworth. The original building was demolished and rebuilt in 1737, possibly to a design by Leoni, the designer of the house, for the tenth Peter Legh. It is constructed of sandstone rubble with ashlar sandstone dressings. The four-square, three-storey building has small, square towers surmounted by cupolas at the corners.

The park was originally enclosed in the 14th century by the first Piers Legh. A large herd of red deer descended from the original herd still live in the grounds, alongside a small herd of shaggy-coated Highland cattle.

The present Lyme Park house dates from the latter part of the 16th century, and alterations were made to it in the 1720s by Giacomo Leoni, who retained some of the Elizabethan features and added the courtyard and the south range. Formal gardens, including Mr Darcy's lake, were created in the late 19th and early 20th centuries.

Address Lyme Park, Disley, Stockport, SK12 2NR, www.nationaltrust.org.uk/visit/cheshire-greater-manchester/lyme | **Getting there** Signposted off the A6 Whaley Bridge to Stockport road | **Hours** See website for seasonal opening hours | **Tip** A visit to Mr Darcy's Pemberley (the house at Lyme Park) would be an excellent finale to a trip to The Cage. There is a National Trust car park, café, coffee shop and second-hand bookshop in the house.

9 Cup and Ring Rock

A Neolithic mystery

Mysterious cup and ring marks are a form of prehistoric art which is particularly found in northern England and on the Atlantic seaboard of Europe. They consist of concave depressions (or cups), pecked into a rock surface and often surrounded by concentric circles (the rings) etched into the stone.

Dating from the Neolithic period (perhaps as much as 10,000 years ago) they are known to archaeologists as petroglyphs. They are found on natural boulders and outcrops and also on megalithic monuments such as stone circles and passage graves. But the intriguing fact is that even today no one can be exactly sure what they represent.

The large, earthfast boulder found above Gardom's Edge above Baslow is the finest example of a cup-and-ring carved rock in the Peak District. Others exist at Rowtor Rocks, near Birchover. Discovered in the 1960s, the Gardom's Edge design consists of a series of cup and ring marks together with a small spiral and two circles that enclose multiple cup marks.

But the 'rock' we see today is a fibreglass replica and not the original, which was reburied to preserve it and to protect it from weathering. Another replica is in the Weston Park Museum in Sheffield.

Recent archaeological investigations have discovered that the area around Gardom's and Birchen Edges was well populated and cultivated as early as the third and second millennia (during the Neolithic and Bronze Ages). Clearance cairns and field systems are signs of a thriving agricultural community.

And just within the spindly birch trees towards Gardom's Edge stands a leaning, triangular, seven-foot-high monolith which may have been an astronomical marker, as the orientation and inclination of the stone is aligned to the altitude of the sun at midsummer. It is believed that the monolith was set in place to give symbolic meaning to the location through the changing seasons.

Address Gardom's Edge between the A617 and the A621 | Getting there Take the footpath from The Robin Hood Inn (DE45 1PQ) on the A619 Baslow to Chesterfield road | Hours Accessible 24 hours | Tip The Robin Hood Inn (+44 (0) 1629 700888) is a good place to start and finish your walk with a pint or meal in a welcoming, family and walker-friendly pub.

10 Curbar Edge

Filming on the Edge

When TV and film companies are looking for easily accessible locations for filming spots with great views, they usually head for Curbar Edge. Reached by a short walk and very little effort, the views from Curbar Edge are some of the finest in the Peak District, extending south down the Derwent Valley towards the parklands of Chatsworth, west across to the White Peak and the villages of Stoney Middleton and Eyam, and north towards Stanage Edge and the higher moors above Hathersage.

Curbar Edge also has some outstanding rock features, formed from the clerical grey gritstone which characterises the Eastern Edges. Prominent among these is the isolated tower known as Froggatt Pinnacle, first climbed by the pioneering Sheffield rock climber J. W. Puttrell in 1900. Puttrell, with his friends in the Kyndwr Club, also made many of the first ascents of the 230 climbing routes that the Edge now boasts. One of the most challenging of these is the aptly named Peapod, which looks exactly like its name and is graded 'Hard Very Severe'.

The moors behind Curbar Edge contain a wealth of prehistoric remains, including burial cairns, field systems and settlement sites, most dating from the Bronze Age. Herds of red deer are also frequently observed on these moors between Curbar and White Edges.

The Romans are believed to have been the first to exploit the natural gritstone resources of Curbar Edge, which is crossed at Curbar Gap by a Roman road that was turned into a turnpike in 1759. There is an old, badly eroded guide stoop by the side of the car park that dates from that time. Small quarries at Curbar Edge also produced millstones until the early 19th century, when imported composite and burr stones from France hastened the end of the local industry.

Address Curbar Gap car park, Clodhall Lane, Curbar, S32 3YR | Getting there Car park sits above Curbar village via Bar Road and Clodhall Lane, off the A623 Baslow to Calver Road | Hours Accessible 24 hours | Tip On the right of the minor road leading up from the village on the path from Baslow are the Cundy Graves, where Thomas and Ada Cundy and their children were victims of the plague of 1632, 30 years before the more famous Plague visitation at neighbouring Eyam. Each has a slab carved with their initials.

11 Darley Dale Yew Tree

Oldest living thing in the Peak?

Enclosed within iron railings, as if it needed to be restrained, in the churchyard of St Helen's Church at Darley Dale, is the Darley Dale yew tree – probably the oldest living thing in the Peak District.

An estimated 2,000 years old, it witnessed the construction of the 12th-century church it still shelters by its south porch and stands 50 feet high. Its massive, gnarled and fibrous girth measures 35 feet at 4 feet from the ground, and is marked by stone tablets around its trunk commemorating important events during World War Two.

According to the notice attached to the railings, it may also have witnessed Romans building up the funeral pyres for their dead and Saxons converting to Christianity under its ample shade. The large round stone near the chancel door is thought to be the lid of a Roman funeral pyre, and certainly there are some Saxon stone coffin lids in the south porch of the church. The remains of a Saxon preaching cross were also discovered during an 1854 restoration.

St Helen's, which takes its unusual dedication from the mother of Constantine, who became the first Christian Roman Emperor, is an interesting church in its own right. It has elements of architecture from the Norman to the Perpendicular Gothic periods and is notable for the recumbent effigy in the nave of a praying cross-legged knight holding a heart. This is believed to be Sir John de Darley, who was described in a document of 1309 as Governor of Peak Castle at Castleton.

There is also a memorial window to the engineer Sir Joseph Whitworth, who lived at Stancliffe Hall and is buried in the churchyard. The south window is by Edward Burne-Jones and depicts scenes from the Song of Solomon. Two Early English windows on the east side of St Chad's Chapel depict St Helen and St Chad.

The stone screen, dating from the late 14th or early 15th century, is believed to have once enclosed the south transept to form a chapel as a so-called parclose screen.

Address St Helen's Church, Church Road, Darley Dale, DE4 2GG | Getting there Just off the A6 Matlock to Bakewell road | Hours Accessible 24 hours | Tip Beautifully situated on the banks of the River Derwent in Station Road, Darley Dale, is the Square and Compass pub (+44 (0) 1629 733255), which is a friendly village inn catering for locals and visitors alike, and also has a camping and caravan site.

12 Derwent Dams

The drowned villages

Water engineers had their eyes on the Upper Derwent Valley for decades before work began on the initial Howden Dam in 1901. It was the perfect spot: a long deep valley in solid millstone grit, bleak rain-soaked moors all around, close to the thirsty cities, and the need for only a few scattered farming communities to be relocated.

After Howden came the Derwent Dam, built in a similar, battlemented Gothic style, which was completed in 1916. Ladybower, the last and largest, was finished in 1945, flooding two miles of the Derwent Valley and drowning the two ancient villages of Derwent and Ashopton. Homes were dismantled and the villagers transferred to a new housing estate at Yorkshire Bridge, Bamford.

The thousand or so navvies who built the dams, and their families, were housed in a temporary village at Birchinlee, whose corrugated iron roofs and walls gave it the local nickname of Tin Town. Tin Town even had its own shops, community centre, and football and cricket teams which competed in local leagues.

A memorial cross in Bamford churchyard commemorates the 58 former residents of Birchinlee who were reinterred from Derwent churchyard here when the Ladybower Reservoir was constructed.

Ladybower now holds about 6,000 million gallons of water, the others slightly less; more than a third of the contained water is piped to Leicester, another third to Sheffield, and the rest is shared between the East Midland cities of Derby and Nottingham.

In times of drought, thousands flock to see the revealed foundations of the drowned village of Derwent. The only structure to cheat the flood was the ancient packhorse bridge at Derwent, which was dismantled and rebuilt further up the valley to span the infant river at Slippery Stones after the Ladybower Reservoir was opened. It is dedicated to the pioneering Sheffield rambler and guidebook author John Derry.

Address Fairholmes car park, Bamford, Hope Valley, S33 0AQ | **Getting there** The Derwent Dam and Fairholmes car park is signposted on the minor road leading north off the A57 Sheffield to Glossop road | **Hours** Accessible 24 hours | **Tip** Nothing remains today of the former navvies' village of Tin Town, but it's a pleasant, easy four-mile walk around the northern arm of the Ladybower Reservoir from Fairholmes, or up the valley to the Howden Reservoir.

13 Derwent Valley Mills

Birthplace of the Industrial Revolution

It's no exaggeration to say that the lower Derwent Valley was the birthplace of the Industrial Revolution. The series of cotton spinning mills built by Richard Arkwright and others saw the genesis of the factory system, which required buildings to house the revolutionary new water-powered technology for spinning cotton.

It was the first time that large-scale industrial production had been introduced into what had previously been a remote, rural landscape. The need to provide housing and other facilities for workers and managers also resulted in the creation of an exceptional industrial landscape that has retained its qualities over two centuries.

All this was recognised at the meeting of the UNESCO World Heritage Committee in Helsinki in December 2001, when the Derwent Valley Mills was inscribed as a World Heritage Site (WHS). The committee decided that the proposed site met the tests of 'authenticity in design, materials, workmanship, setting and the distinctive character of its industrial landscape components'.

It was Richard Arkwright, a Preston-born barber and wig maker, who first saw the potential of the mighty River Derwent. He invented the water frame, and his 1771 mill at Cromford was the first to utilise water power. An enlightened employer, he also created a village with social amenities for his workforce.

Other mills followed, from Derby north to places like Belper, Milford and Darley Abbey, which now form the heart of the WHS. The Cromford Mills site now forms the centrepiece and Visitor Gateway, where a film and guided tours help you to plan your visit. There are also children's activities, craft shops, a gallery, and food shops.

Here you can also discover more about this unique valley through interactive displays, meet 'Sir Richard' himself in the 'Arkwright Experience', or take a narrowboat ride along the Cromford Canal. This short section is also now an SSSI and local nature reserve.

Address Sir Richard Arkwright's Cromford Mills, Mill Lane, Cromford, Matlock, DE4 3RQ, +44 (0) 1629 823256, www.cromfordmills.org.uk/visit | Getting there On the A6 Derby to Matlock Road, about two miles south of Matlock | Hours Check website for seasonal opening hours | Tip The Cromford Canal Wharf in Mill Road, Cromford, DE4 3RQ, includes the Gothic Warehouse, Wheatcroft's Wharf Café and The Counting House Coffee Stop.

14 Doll Tor

A magical stone circle

Flowers and other offerings are often to be found decorating the site of Doll Tor, a charming little Bronze Age stone circle in a pine woodland clearing west of Stanton Moor near Birchover.

Doll Tor consists of six upright stones arranged in a rough circle with a diameter of 23 feet. A stone cairn was added to the east of the circle, and excavation has revealed that the cremated human remains of several adults and children were buried both within the circle and around the cairn. To the north of the cairn was a pit containing the remains of a probably male adult. A red faience star bead, possibly of Egyptian origin, was found with the bones.

The prolific local antiquarian and so-called 'barrow knight' Thomas Bateman was the first to investigate the site in 1852. Local antiquarians J. P. Heathcote and his son J. C. Heathcote, of Birchover, conducted further excavations between 1931 and 1933, discovering at least six interments of human remains around the cairn to the east of the circle.

But by the early 21st century, the site was being used for ritual activity by modern Pagans, who damaged the officially protected site by increasing the number of stones from six to fourteen and by moving others around. They have subsequently all been returned to their original locations and two formerly prostrate stones have been re-erected. The monument is now said to be closer to its prehistoric appearance than at any time since its construction.

Doll Tor stands on the western flank of Stanton Moor, half a mile north of the village of Birchover. It is close to a range of other prehistoric remains, including the Nine Ladies Stone Circle and the isolated, cup-marked Andle Stone on Stanton Moor, and it overlooks the Harthill Moor Stone Circle.

Doll Tor still exerts a magical atmosphere, which is sometimes missing from more famous stone circles.

Address what3words: layered.rebounder.bottom (for the village of Stanton-in-the-Peak) | **Getting there** At the northern end of the plantation on the west side of the B5056 from Birchover to Stanton-in-the-Peak, about 300 yards from the road | **Hours** Accessible 24 hours | **Tip** If rock climbing is your bag, then there are some bouldering routes on the scattered rocks in the woods below the Doll Tor circle, with imaginative names such as The Doll's House, Dollfin, Dolly Parton and Dollywood.

15 Eagle Stone

Climbing to matrimony

Local tradition claims that eligible young men in the village of Baslow had to climb the 20-foot-high Eagle Rock on Baslow Edge in order to prove themselves worthy of marriage. The rock is severely undercut on all sides, and it was never going to be a particularly easy ascent, so there must have been many Baslow bachelors.

The name of the isolated gritstone tor has nothing to do with the 'King of the Birds', the fearsome raptor of the Scottish Highlands, but is said to be a corruption of the name of Aigle, a pagan Celtic deity well known for his habit of throwing large stones. And, if you use a little imagination, you can still see the square-jawed profile of a giant's head in the stone. Another explanation is that the name derives from the Egglestone, or witches', stone.

In common with isolated rocks elsewhere, many legends surround the Eagle Stone. For example, on certain mornings of the year, the stone is said to get up and take a walk around the moors and, according to *Household Tales* by Sidney Oldhall Addy (1895), the Eagle Stone turns around whenever it hears a cock crow.

Recent archaeological research has shown that the area around the Eagle Stone was a centre of prehistoric activity. At least eight phases of activity, extending over several hundreds of years during the Bronze Age, have been identified, including clearance cairns, stone platforms and low field walls.

Close to the Eagle Stone is the Wellington Monument, erected in 1866 by a local Dr Wrench to commemorate the Duke of Wellington's victory at the Battle of Waterloo in 1815.

An added bonus in your short walk up from the Curbar Gap car park in recent years has been the chance of meeting up with a herd of beautiful, shaggy, ginger-coated Highland cattle that the National Trust has been employing to graze the moorland behind Baslow Edge. There's no chance of seeing a golden eagle on the stone, though…

Address The Eagle Stone, Baslow Edge, Baslow | **Getting there** From the Curbar Gap car park (S32 3YR), the main path along Baslow Edge leads straight to the Eagle Stone | **Hours** Accessible 24 hours | **Tip** The Wheatsheaf at Nether End, Baslow (+44 (0) 1246 582240) is a former 18th-century coaching house located on the edge of Chatsworth Park by the River Derwent, and is handy for a pint after your exploration of Baslow Edge.

16 Edensor

The 'transplanted' village

The popular story goes that the Chatsworth estate village of Edensor (pronounced 'En-zer') was literally transplanted by the 6th Duke of Devonshire because it spoilt the view from his stately home. Until the 1760s, the original village spread over the flat ground west of the house to the River Derwent.

But that tale was roundly denied by Deborah, the late 11th Duchess of Devonshire, in her 1990 book, *The Estate,* in which she said it was 'unproven and to my mind unlikely'. She continued: '…firstly because it would have been out of character with the 6th Duke, who liked his fellow men, and secondly because the lie of the land meant that only two or three houses could have been seen.'

A second story – that the 6th Duke chose the jumble of architectural styles that made Edensor such an oddity among English villages, from an architectural pattern book – is apparently closer to the truth. The Duke employed architectural draughtsman John Robertson with the task of committing the Duke's idiosyncratic choice of a mixture of styles into stone and mortar.

The result, according to the 19th-century garden designer John Claudius Loudon, was that the Edensor cottages 'present a perfect compendium of all the prettiest cottage styles from the sturdy Norman to the sprightly Italian'. Others have suggested that the almost theatrical mishmash of styles – from Norman villa to Tudor, Jacobean, Italianate and Swiss Alpine cottages – pays no regard to the local vernacular, apart from the fact that they are all built in local gritstone. The 30-odd cottages are mostly lived in by staff working at the nearby Big House.

The tall and elegant spire of St Peter's parish church at Edensor, which stands at the top of the village, was designed by Sir George Gilbert Scott, restorer of so many other churches, and was consecrated in 1870.

Address Edensor, Bakewell, DE45 1PH | **Getting there** On the minor road that runs through Chatsworth Park between Rowsley and Baslow | **Hours** Accessible 24 hours; cottages viewable from the outside only | **Tip** The Edensor Tea Cottage (+44 (0) 1246 582315) in the main street is the ideal place to enjoy a cuppa after exploring the village and house. It provides great, locally produced food and a very warm and friendly service.

17 Errwood Hall

A romantic ruin

The starkly beautiful remains of Errwood Hall, standing high in a wooded glen above the reservoirs of the Goyt Valley, are surely one of the most romantic ruins in the Peak District. Particularly gorgeous in the early summer, when the thousands of rhododendron and azalea shrubs are in glorious full bloom, the ruins tell the story of a once thriving community built on the wealth of a Manchester industrialist.

Errwood Hall was an Italianate mansion built by Samuel Grimshaw in 1830. Grimshaw made his fortune in shipping and property and owned his own yacht, the *Mariquita*. He employed 20 servants at Errwood, and the family was known for the lavish parties held there, especially during the shooting season.

Grimshaw planted between 40,000 and 50,000 rhododendrons and azaleas around his estate between 1840 and 1850, and from the end of the 19th century, in an early example of opening the grounds to the public, he welcomed them on Tuesdays and Saturdays.

Above the house on the top of the hill is the fenced private burial ground of the Grimshaws, which once also boasted a small mausoleum, now demolished. The magnificent view from here extends over the hall ruins to the reservoirs below and to the hills above Buxton.

Above the burial ground is the circular, pine-sheltered shrine to St Joseph, erected in 1889 by the family in memory of Miss Dolores de Ybarguen, the aristocratic Spanish companion to Grimshaw's wife Jesse, who died on a visit to Lourdes in her 40s. Flowers are always to be found on the altar in the shrine.

After a short period as a youth hostel, Errwood Hall was partially demolished when the Fernilee Reservoir was built in 1937 by Stockport Corporation. Errwood Reservoir followed in 1967 and the hamlet of Goyt's Bridge disappeared under the water, although the packhorse bridge was saved and re-erected in 1965 over Wildmoorstone Brook further up the valley.

Address Goyt Valley, SK17 6GJ | **Getting there** Derbyshire Bridge car park signposted from the Macclesfield to Buxton A537 road (SK17 6TT); the ruins of the hall are a short walk away | **Hours** Accessible 24 hours | **Tip** The Errwood Sailing Club (Errwood Reservoir, Sandy Lane, Buxton, SK17 6GJ) was founded in November 1968 shortly after the construction of the reservoir. It is one of the few reservoirs in the Peak District that offers various sailing, windsurfing and powerboat training courses throughout the year.

18 Eyam Village Stocks

Don't become a laughing stock!

If you were unemployed, asking for higher wages, caught begging, swearing or the worse the wear for drink in medieval England, you could find yourself confined to the stocks on the village green for a few days. Once you were restrained with your feet firmly held in the padlocked footholds, fellow villagers would hurl insults or rotten vegetables, or – worse still – remove your shoes and tickle your feet. You'd literally become the village laughing stock! You can still see sets of village stocks in the Peak District on the village greens at Eyam and Litton and in Chapel-en-le-Frith's Market Place.

Stocks became common in England by the 14th century when in 1351, the Statute of Labourers was passed, requiring every town to provide and maintain a set of stocks. This was believed to be a reaction to the Black Death, which halved the population – the consequent scarcity of labour encouraged farm workers to demand increased pay. The law aimed to discourage this by providing that anyone demanding (or offering) higher wages should be set in the stocks for up to three days.

Stocks were also used to control the unemployed, beggars and the poor. The Vagabonds and Beggars Act of 1494 provided that 'vagabonds, idle and suspected persons' should be set in the stocks for three days and nights and have no sustenance other than bread and water. The Poor Law Act of 1531 directed that vagabonds should be licensed to beg, and beggars if found begging should be whipped or put in the stocks for three days and nights.

A law of 1605 required that anyone convicted of drunkenness should receive six hours in the stocks, and those convicted of being a drunkard (as opposed to just being caught drunk) should suffer four hours in the stocks or pay the substantial fine of three shillings and six pence (about £32 today). A slightly later statute made it legal to set those caught swearing in the stocks for one hour, if they would not pay a fine of one shilling (just over £9 today).

Address On Eyam village green opposite Eyam Hall, S32 5QW | **Getting there** Just off the A623 Baslow to Peak Forest road | **Hours** Accessible 24 hours | **Tip** Jacobean Eyam Hall (+44 (0) 1433 350055) built in 1672, just six years after the plague, has been in the Wright family for 350 years and is well worth a visit.

19 Footpath Sign, Hayfield

Signing the way for 130 years

In 1894 – the year that William Ewart Gladstone was serving his last term as Liberal prime minister, the Manchester Ship Canal was opened by Queen Victoria, and both Tower Bridge and Blackpool Tower were completed – a meeting in Manchester saw the birth of the oldest and still most active footpath society in Britain.

The Peak District and Northern Counties Footpaths Preservation Society was founded in August of that year at a meeting in the Young Men's Christian Association Hall, Peter Street, Manchester. It came at a time when the advent of steam-driven trains was seeing ever greater numbers of people travelling out into the countryside for walking and recreation, only to be met by signs on the Peak District moors threatening that 'Trespassers will be Prosecuted'.

So one of the first major achievements of 'the Peak & Northern' – as the society is affectionately known – was gaining agreement for public access from local grouse moor owners to the route over Kinder Scout between Hayfield and the former Snake Inn. Its actions enabled the Snake Path, originally an ancient packhorse route, to become a public right of way, as the sign says, 'for ever'.

Two years after the founding of the Peak & Northern, its first (wooden) signpost was planted on this route, replaced in 1906 by the present familiar, green-painted cast-iron sign in Kinder Road, Hayfield. Thirty-five years after the route was established, things hadn't improved that much, and the same path saw the start of the celebrated Mass Trespass on Kinder Scout, which saw five ramblers imprisoned for exercising their 'right to roam'.

In 1968 it was agreed to shorten the Society's name to the Peak and Northern Footpaths Society. Today the Peak & Northern is still the longest surviving regional footpath society in the UK, with more than 1,400 members, and it has erected no fewer than 563 signposts like that at Hayfield, and 47 bridges.

Address Kinder Road, Hayfield, High Peak, SK22 2LE | Getting there Kinder Road is a minor road leading east from Hayfield village centre | Hours Accessible 24 hours | Tip Just off the Kinder Road to the right about half a mile from the P&NFS sign is Bowden Bridge, a charming 18th-century packhorse bridge across the River Kinder.

20 Forest Chapel

An ancient tradition

In the days before tiling or carpeting were commonplace and most buildings had earthen floors, the floor covering in village churches often took the form of rushes taken from the nearby fields and used as a form of renewable 'carpeting'. The tradition of replacing those rushes is known as rushbearing and is still practised in a few village churches in the north of England, such as in the 17th-century Forest Chapel at Macclesfield Forest on the western edge of the Peak District National Park. The well-attended annual rushbearing ceremony at Forest Chapel usually takes place on the first Sunday after 12 August.

The chapel originally served the medieval Royal Forest of Macclesfield, which was a hunting reserve owned by the Earls of Chester and formerly stretched from the foothills of the Pennines east into the High Peak near Whaley Bridge and south to the Staffordshire Moorlands. The modern commercial forest is owned by United Utilities, and most is designated a Site of Biological Importance. The area around Trentabank Reservoir is a nature reserve managed by the Cheshire Wildlife Trust and contains one of the largest heronries in the district.

Dedicated to St Stephen, Forest Chapel was built in 1673 as a chapel of ease for Prestbury and became the church for the parish of Macclesfield Forest and Wildboarclough in 1906. While the core of the building is late 17th century, the chapel was completely rebuilt in 1834. The interior is simple, with whitewashed walls and plain Victorian furnishings and pews. A benefaction board records that in 1796 Edmund Brough of Worcester bequeathed the interest on £100 to be given to the poor of the parish every Candlemas Day, but 'not to any of the poor who have any relief from the parish'.

Both of the highest points in Cheshire are close by: Shining Tor, the highest at 1,834 feet, can be seen from the forest; and Shutlingsloe, at 1,669 feet, also overlooks the forest and is dubbed 'the Matterhorn of Cheshire'.

Address St Stephen's Church, Oven Lane, Macclesfield Forest, SK11 0AR, www.rainowchurches.org/forest-chapel | Getting there Off the A537 Buxton to Macclesfield road just after the former Cat & Fiddle public house | Hours See website for details | Tip While birdwatchers will love the Trentabank Nature Reserve (Standing Stone Road, Langley, SK11 0NS), it is also home to a number of other animals including badgers, weasels and red deer, although you will be lucky to see them.

21 Guide Stoop, Beeley Moor

Guiding the way

The Peak District is covered by a network of ancient packhorse routes, which were the motorways of their day and major arteries for the commercial transportation of goods by trains of packhorses. But in the days before road signs, maps and Satnav, navigation across the bleak, uninhabited moorland of the Peak District could be very difficult, especially in winter when the not infrequent mist, rain or snow set in.

The answer was the erection of stone guideposts – locally known as stoops (from a Scandinavian word for stone) – which indicated the way for the weary traveller across what Daniel Defoe dubbed in his 1725 *Journey Through Britain* as a 'howling wilderness', and 'the most desolate, wild and abandoned country in all England'.

Guideposts were erected mainly in the north of England from the early 18th century to comply with an Act of Parliament of 1697 that required directional stones to be put up at road junctions in remote moorland areas, where travellers would be likely to go astray.

About 50 were erected in Derbyshire, and the majority have inscriptions on four sides indicating the direction of the nearest market towns. The spelling on guide stoops varies considerably, usually preserving an approximation of the local vernacular. Examples of this are signs to the nearby city of Sheffield, which is spelt Shafild, Shefild and Sheaffield among eight different versions. Alfreton is variously spelt Offerton, Allforton and Alfarton, while Hathersage appears as Hatharsich. These spellings may well reflect local pronunciations.

Most of the stoops have the names carved in capital letters, and many also have carved hands with fingers pointing in the directions of the various destinations.

The version featured here stands near Hell Bank Plantation on Beeley Moor, and the spelling is pretty accurate, pointing to 'roades' to Bakewell, Chesterfield, Chatsworth and Offerton (Alfreton).

Address Beeley Moor, what3words: radiates.topping.glitz | **Getting there** Just off the minor road between Beeley and Holymoorside on the sharp bend at the eastern end of Hell Bank Plantation | **Hours** Accessible 24 hours | **Tip** Beeley is a Chatsworth estate village, and characterful The Beeley Inn in the village square (+44 (0) 1629 733259) was converted to an inn in 1747.

22 Holme Moss Mast

Highest and most powerful

The sight of the often cloud-capped 750-foot mast of the transmitting station on the 1,719-foot summit of Holme Moss, on the border of the Peak District and West Yorkshire, must have been met with considerable relief by cyclists taking part in the Tour de France in 2014.

Nicknamed by the cyclists 'Le Col de Moss', it is a gruelling four-mile, 1,293-foot climb up from Holmfirth in the Holme Valley with an average gradient of 5.6 per cent, although the penultimate kilometre has a gradient of a formidable 11 per cent. It has gained a reputation as one of the country's most arduous climbs and is also regularly used during the Tour of Britain and other biking events.

The Holme Moss transmitting station itself is the highest and most powerful VHF station in England. Weighing 140 tons, it is supported by five enormous sets of stays. These often become coated with heavy ice in the winter, which has to be removed before it brings the towering structure crashing down.

The original Holme Moss transmitting station was commissioned in 1951 and VHF radio broadcasts started in 1956. The mast survived until the end of the Band 1 TV broadcasts in 1985, and the present sky-scraping VHF mast was constructed to take over from the original in 1984.

The mast provides VHF coverage for FM and DAB to a wide area including West Yorkshire, South Yorkshire, Greater Manchester and parts of Derbyshire, Cheshire and Nottinghamshire. Reception is also available as far north as Scotland, as far south as London and to the east and west coasts. Coverage can also be picked up in Ireland and even in mainland Europe.

Near the car park at the Holme Moss summit, a sadly rusted metal picture frame shows the magnificent view east across West and South Yorkshire, with the message: 'Framing the Landscape: Many people look but only a few see.'

Address Holme Moss, Holmfirth, HD9 2QF | Getting there The A6024 road between Holmfirth and Longdendale crosses the moor near its highest point close to Holme Moss | Hours Viewable 24 hours | Tip Holmfirth, the village below Holme Moss, was the setting for *Last of the Summer Wine*, one of the longest-running BBC TV sitcoms, which ran for 31 series from 1973 to 2010. You can still enjoy a cuppa in their favourite meeting place, Sid's Café in Towngate (+44 (0) 7706 823855).

23 The Hunting Tower

Where Bess watched the hunt

Lady Elizabeth Cavendish – better known today as Bess of Hardwick – is usually credited, with her second husband Sir William Cavendish, with the building of the first Chatsworth House in mid 16th century.

Little now remains of that original Tudor mansion, gradually replaced over a 20-year period in the 17th century by the 4th Earl (later the 1st Duke) of Devonshire and architect William Talman. Today's gilded and Palladian-fronted 'Palace of the Peak' is instantly recognisable as one of the most famous and popular stately homes in England.

But one building proudly remains from Bess's original house – the Hunting Tower in Stand Wood, overlooking the house by a lofty 400 feet. The triangular, turreted four-storey building was designed by the renowned Elizabethan architect Robert Smythson and completed for Bess around 1583. The Hunting Tower was probably used as a banqueting hall or summerhouse but, as its name implies, its primary purpose was for spectators watching the hounds and huntsmen pursuing their quarry of red and fallow deer in the parkland below.

The modern visitor can enjoy the same contrasting views to the west as Bess's guests, with its planned landscape, including the house and formal gardens, later extensively redesigned for the 6th Duke by Joseph Paxton, and the Lancelot 'Capability' Brown parkland beyond, where red and fallow deer still graze.

Inside the tower, a steep spiral staircase provides access to the four floors, with each room echoing the unusual exterior shape of the building. The Tower is now let as holiday accommodation by the Chatsworth Estate.

The Hunting tower is reached via a series of signposted footpaths and trails through Stand Wood, and the ever-increasing views of the park and house are worth the steep climb.

Address Chatsworth Hunting Tower, Chatsworth, Bakewell, DE45 1PN | Getting there Well signposted from the A6 and A619 heading towards Bakewell | Hours Viewable from the outside only | Tip A first-time trip to the Peak District would probably not be complete without a visit to its most famous and popular stately home, Chatsworth House. A treasure house of works of art, it remains the home of the 12th Duke of Devonshire and his family (+44 (0) 1246 565300).

24 Little John's Grave

Last resting place of Robin's loyal lieutenant?

Whether Robin Hood and his Merry Men ever really existed remains a much-loved – and frequently filmed – legend, but which unfortunately is not based on any conclusive historical facts. Rather like King Arthur and his Knights of the Round Table, Robin and his Merry Men remain akin to medieval superheroes, much exploited by the filmmakers of Hollywood.

Robin's loyal lieutenant Little John has always been an essential part of the story, first recorded in William Langland's *Vision of Piers Plowman* written in the second half of the 14th century. His name is a typically English ironic reference to his huge frame, as he is usually portrayed as a gigantic figure – a seven-foot-tall master of the quarterstaff. In folklore, on their first meeting, he fights and beats Robin Hood on a fallen tree bridge across a river, suitably impressing the outlaw leader.

By tradition, Little John was a nailor hailing from the Hope Valley village of Hathersage, which has a tradition of nail and pin-making, and where his massive grave in St Michael and All Saint's churchyard still attracts curious visitors. A relatively modern tombstone sheltered by an ancient, clipped yew today marks the grave, which lies just outside the church porch. It states that John died in a cottage east of the churchyard while another stone states that the care of the grave was appropriately taken over by the Ancient Order of Foresters Friendly Society in 1929. Local histories also state that Little John's longbow and cap were on display inside St Michael's Church in 1652.

Whether Little John was ever actually interred here remains tantalisingly unproven, though when the grave was excavated in 1784, a thigh bone measuring 30 inches long was uncovered. This suggests a very tall man of up to eight feet in height. Who knows? And there's a Robin Hood's Cave on nearby Stanage Edge.

Address St Michael and All Saints Parish Church, Church Bank, Hathersage, Hope Valley, S32 1AJ | **Getting there** A 10-minute walk from the centre of Hathersage. Walk east along the main road and follow School Lane northward; the slightly steeper Church Bank, on the left, leads to the church | **Hours** Grave accessible 24 hours; church open daily during daylight hours | **Tip** If you fancy a quick dip, the heated outdoor Hathersage Swimming Pool in Oddfellows Road (+44 (0) 1433 650843) is open all year round and has a café for a hot drink afterwards.

25 Longdendale Reservoirs

Water from heaven

At the time of their construction in the mid to late 19th century, the string of five reservoirs which flood the Longdendale valley in the far north of the Peak District were the largest expanse of artificial water in the world.

The reservoirs – running for seven miles east from the upper end of the valley: the Woodhead, Torside, Rhodeswood, Valehouse and Bottoms – were desperately needed to slake the ever-growing thirst of the fast-expanding industrial cities of Manchester and Stockport. And they were the brainchild of one man – John Frederick Bateman, a respected civil engineer and a member of the Royal Society, later to become the president of the Institution of Civil Engineers.

The River Etherow, which rises in the Black Cloughs on the northern slopes of the 2,000-foot moorland plateau of Bleaklow, south of Longdendale, was the source of this soon-to-be-exploited water. It was described by Bateman as 'The water… which may be collected in reservoirs constructed for this purpose, will be nearly as pure as it comes from heaven'.

The first dam to be constructed was the Woodhead, the highest of the string of five, which was started in 1848, but it was not to be completed until 1877 because of unexpected flooding due to geological difficulties. The nearly two-mile-long Mottram Tunnel, which was to take the water to Manchester and Tameside, was also begun in 1848, while work on the Rhodeswood and Torside Reservoirs began in 1849 and the Valehouse and Bottoms later, in 1865 and 1867 respectively.

The largest completed reservoir was the Woodhead, which covered 135 acres and had a capacity of 1,181 million gallons, while the smallest was the Valehouse, which contained only 342 million gallons. The project was completed in 1877 at a cost of over £3 million, and now supplies Manchester with 24 million gallons of water every day.

Address Crowden (SK13 1HZ) | **Getting there** Longdendale on the A628 Sheffield to Glossop road | **Hours** Accessible 24 hours | **Tip** The Bull's Head in Old Road, Tintwistle (pronounced 'Tinsel'), is a traditional country pub situated just beyond Bottoms Reservoir at the western end of Longdendale.

26 Mam Tor, Castleton

The Shivering Mountain

Mam Tor, the 1,695-foot so-called 'Shivering Mountain', standing sentinel at the head of the Hope Valley above Castleton, was recently placed in the top 10 in a survey of Britain's 100 favourite walks.

The breathtaking views from the top are some of the finest in the Peak. They extend down the Great Ridge path towards Lose Hill, north across the Vale of Edale to the plateau of Kinder Scout, and east to the Derwent Moors and the long gritstone wall of Stanage Edge. Castle-crowned Castleton, the Winnats Pass and the cement works chimney at Hope are to the south, with the limestone plateau of the White Peak rolling away in the background.

Mam Tor is known as the Shivering Mountain not because of its ambient temperature but because of the constant landslips in the shales on its east face, memorably described by 17th-century traveller Celia Fiennes '...in resemblance as a great Hay-Ricke that's cut down one halfe...'.

It is also the site of one of the highest and largest hillforts in the Pennines and one of the few to be excavated by archaeologists. In the mid 1960s a Manchester University dig produced a wealth of fresh information about the fort, including pottery and several hut circles. Two Bronze Age barrows were also discovered on the summit, the highest of which the National Trust has encapsulated in cobbles to ensure its preservation. There was also an earlier settlement enclosed by the ramparts, and several circular houses or huts were built on terraced platforms on the upper slopes of the hill. Archaeologists believe that the fort might have been built as a summer shelter for herdsmen using the hills for grazing their animals, but it might also have had a strategic military purpose or been built simply to overawe a neighbouring tribe.

Today it is the haunt of hang gliders and paragliders, who soar in the thermals over the Hope Valley like latter-day pterodactyls.

Address Mam Tor National Trust car park, S33 8WA | Getting there Off the A625 Castleton to Chapel-en-le-Frith road, about a mile west of Castleton | Hours Accessible 24 hours | Tip It's worth taking a short walk from Mam Tor summit along the now-paved Great Ridge walk towards Hollins Cross and Back Tor. The views towards Kinder Scout to the north and down the Hope Valley to the south are spectacular.

27 Millennium Bridge

The missing link

In 1996, Councillor Martin Doughty was faced with an apparently intractable problem over which he'd been agonising for 20 years. As the youngest ever New Mills town councillor and now the livewire leader of Derbyshire County Council, he had been instrumental in the creation of the Torrs Riverside Park, which followed the winding course of the River Goyt as it snaked below the former mill town in a deep gorge.

But there was a 'missing link' between the western entrance to the gorge and New Mills Central railway station, and main Torrs Riverside Park and the confluence of the Goyt with the River Sett.

The northern side of the gorge was hemmed in by a gigantic curving Victorian railway retaining wall – said to be the largest in the country – below the New Mills Junction on the railway above. Would it be possible to build a walkway 20 feet above the rushing river but attached to that retaining wall?

The design of the 175-yard walkway was critical, and Karl Cooper's sweeping 'steel spider's web' design, attached to the massive, curved retaining wall and cantilevered on slim columns over the river, was the answer. Skilfully engineered by the County Council's project manager Stan Brewster, it was an innovative, exciting and bold solution.

Completed in 1999, the £500,000 walkway provided an important missing link for the Mid Shires Way, allowing people to walk the entire 225-mile trail between Stockport and The Ridgeway in Buckinghamshire.

The elegant bridge will remain a lasting tribute to the vision of the New Mills lad Martin Doughty, who was later knighted and became chairman of English Nature, but who tragically died early at the age of 59 in 2009. Stan Brewster also died tragically young at the age of 52 in the Edgware Road tube station bombings in London in 2005.

Address The Torrs Riverside Park, New Mills, High Peak, SK22 3ES | Getting there From the Torr Top car park in New Mills, take the steps that lead down a short hill to the Millennium Bridge | Hours Accessible 24 hours | Tip A plaque on the wall of the former police station in Hall Street, New Mills records the fact that this is where the five young men arrested during the Mass Trespass on Kinder Scout in April 1932 were first incarcerated.

28 Millstones, Millstone Edge

Millstones round their necks

The millstone is the instantly recognisable symbol of the Peak District National Park. The quarrying and creation of millstones from the eponymous millstone grit of the Dark Peak was an important industry in the region for at least 500 years, the earliest being the domed millstones, which were used for grinding barley and were being made from as early as the 13th century.

The more common flat-edged millstones came later and were used for grinding animal feed and pulpstone for paper manufacture. The stones – more correctly known as grindstones – were quarried and shaped by hand on the spot and then transported off the moorland either in pairs with a linking axle or by sledge to the nearest packhorse route. Then they were taken to the river ports of Bawtry or Stainsforth in Yorkshire and on to Hull, where they were shipped to the south of England via the Humber.

But by the 18th century, the millstone trade had all but collapsed as Continental stones were being imported that produced finer flour to satisfy the nation's taste for whiter bread. Flour created from Derbyshire millstones left a fine stone powder, making it grey and undesirable for human consumption.

Reminders of the once great millstone industry can still be found at places like Bolehill and Millstone Edge quarries and at the southern end of Stanage Edge above Hathersage. Piles of neatly stacked but no longer saleable millstones can still be discovered, some bearing their maker's initials, among the bracken and birches beneath the gritstone edges.

Replacing the original rather Feudal image of Peveril Castle, the millstone became the logo of the Peak District National Park Authority in the 1980s. This reflected the fact that the Peak has always been a living, working landscape, shaped by the people who live and work there.

Address Surprise View car park is off the A625 Sheffield to Hathersage road at S32 1DA | **Getting there** Bolehill Quarry and Millstone Edge quarries are a short walk on either side of the A625 Sheffield to Hathersage road at Surprise View | **Hours** Accessible 24 hours | **Tip** The appropriately named, dog-friendly former coaching inn the Millstone Country Inn, is on the A625 Sheffield Road, above Hathersage (+44 (0) 1433 650258) and offers glorious views down the Hope Valley, just below Surprise View.

29 Moot Hall

Laying down the lead law

Claimed to be one of the oldest courts of law in the country, the Moot Hall in Chapel Lane, Wirksworth, is the home of the Barmote Court, an ancient body that regulates the laws and customs of the formerly important local lead mining industry.

There is no record of the first Barmote Court in Wirksworth, but the Great Barmote Court, covering 'the Low Peak or Soke and Wapentake of Wirksworth', was known to be in existence in 1415.

The court administers laws first laid down in the *Quo Warranto* inquisition, held at Ashbourne in 1288, during the reign of Edward I. The court, consisting of a Chief Barmaster and 12 jurors, still meets once a year in April to determine the allocation of mines and resolve any disputes. Each juror is fed with cheese and beer and presented with a clay pipe to mark their service.

The present Grade II-listed building was built in 1814 at the direction of Charles Bathurst, Chancellor of the Duchy of Lancaster, a major local landowner. It is built in ashlar stone and designed in the neoclassical style, with a façade of three bays. On either side of the front windows are two stone panels recovered from an earlier Moot Hall, depicting lead mining tools including a pair of scales, a pick-axe, a dish and Roman fasces (a bundle of sticks and an axe). Firmly chained inside the hall is a bronze measuring dish, capable of holding about 65 lbs of dressed lead ore, presented by Henry VIII to the Barmote Court in 1513. It was used by court officials to ensure that the volume and weight of the miners' lead ore (galena) conformed to the allowable amounts.

The Barmote Court also acted as a coroner's and criminal court. The harsh penalty for stealing from a mine was to have a hand nailed to the mine's stow (winch), giving the unfortunate accused the unenviable choice of either tearing himself loose – or starving to death.

Thankfully, such a brutal sentence has not been recorded recently.

Address Moot Hall, Chapel Lane, Wirksworth, DE4 4FF, calendarcustoms.com/articles/great-barmote-court | Getting there Just off Coldwell Street in the centre of Wirksworth | Hours Viewable from the outside only, except during court sessions – see website for details | Tip In a former quarry just to the south of Wirksworth, off Porter Lane on the B5036, is the free-to-enter National Stone Centre (+44 (0) 1629 824833), where you can discover how stone is formed and extracted, and its myriad different modern uses.

30 Nelson's Monument

'England expects' on Birchen Edge

Londoners had to wait three long decades before they could permanently commemorate Admiral Lord Horatio Nelson's famous victory at the Battle of Trafalgar in 1805, with William Railton's towering Nelson's Column in Trafalgar Square in the centre of the capital.

Peak District folk, on the other hand, only had to wait five years to see the ball-topped, 10-foot-high column on Birchen Edge overlooking Baslow to be erected in the maritime hero's honour. The man behind the speedy commemoration was local Baslow businessman John Brightman, who oversaw its erection in 1810.

Close to Brightman's column stand three natural rocky tors that were named after three of the ships that took part in the epic battle against the French and Spanish fleets in Trafalgar Bay. The names of the *Victory*, the ship on which Nelson died, the *Royal Soverin* [sic] and the *Defiance* are carved in capital letters into the rocks.

Amusingly, several of the rock climbs on adjacent Birchen Edge also adopt Nelsonian names, such as Kiss me Hardy (said to be Nelson's last words), Emma's Dilemma (Emma Hamilton was Nelson's paramour), The Crow's Nest and the Victory and Trafalgar Cracks and Gulleys.

Just over a mile away, across the A621 Baslow to Sheffield road stands another monument commemorating another Napoleonic war hero. Cross-topped Wellington's Monument on Baslow Edge was erected by local resident Dr Edward Mason Wrench (1833–1912) in 1866 to celebrate the achievements of Arthur Wellesley, Duke of Wellington, victor at the Battle of Waterloo in 1815.

It is believed that Wrench, a former Lieutenant Colonel in the Army, felt that Wellington should receive equal acknowledgement as naval hero Nelson on nearby Birchen Edge. Another story claims that it was built to commemorate Wellington's visit to the Duke of Rutland at Haddon Hall. The 10-foot-high monument was built on a gritstone boulder and now stands as a war memorial to fallen local soldiers.

Address Birchen Edge, DE45 1PQ | Getting there It's a short moorland walk up to the monument from The Robin Hood pub on the A619 Baslow to Chesterfield road | Hours Accessible 24 hours | Tip There are great views down across Baslow village and the Chatsworth estate from the 1,017-foot trig point at the summit of Birchin Edge.

31 North Lees Hall

'Out on the wily, windy moors'

The actual location of Thornfield Hall in *Jane Eyre*, Charlotte Brontë's smouldering and often filmed 1847 blockbuster, has been debated by avid Brontë followers for years.

But by far the favourite candidate for surly Mr Rochester's home is North Lees Hall (private), which shelters below Stanage Edge above Hathersage. It is well attested that Charlotte Brontë (1816–55) paid several visits to North Lees Hall when staying with her friend Ellen Nussey at the vicarage in Hathersage. And her description of the house as 'three storeys high, of proportions not vast, though considerable' – seems to precisely match the Tudor tower house we see today.

The house features a battlemented façade on the west tower, mullioned windows, and an outstanding view from the roof. The Apostles' Chest, a unique item of furniture formerly belonging to the Eyres, is now in the Brontë Museum at Haworth. The legend of a mad woman at North Lees, reputed to have perished in a fire, may also have been the inspiration for Mrs Rochester's dramatic death.

North Lees Hall was built for William Jessop in the last decade of the 16th century, and is ascribed to Robert Smythson, one of the most prominent architects of the Elizabethan era, who was also responsible for Hardwick Hall.

Earlier occupants were the Eyres, a staunchly Roman Catholic local family who lived at North Lees Hall for two generations during the 15th century. They took up the tenancy again in 1750 and lived there until 1882. It is said that Robert Eyre, who lived across the valley at Highlow Hall, built a hall within view of his own home for each of his seven sons, North Lees Hall being one of them.

The quotation which heads this chapter is taken from Kate Bush's 1978 hit single 'Wuthering Heights', written by Bush at the age of 18 after she had read Emily Brontë's equally famous book.

Address Birley Lane, Hathersage, Hope Valley, S32 1DY | **Getting there** From the centre of Hathersage, turn right off the main road into Jaggers Lane. Take the next right into Coggers Lane and follow the lane up the hill for approximately a mile before turning right into Birley Lane | **Hours** Viewable from the outside only | **Tip** The ancient, paved route that ascends neighbouring Stanage Edge – known as the Long Causeway – was long thought to be Roman in origin. But modern archaeology has established that it was more likely a medieval packhorse route linking Sheffield with Hathersage and the Hope Valley.

32 Packhorse Bridge

Bridges over troubled waters

Often described as the motorways of the 17th and 18th centuries, packhorse routes criss-crossed the Peak District carrying goods that ranged from lead to wool and from salt to stone. But they were often faced with the numerous fast-flowing streams and rivers that feed off the moors, so bridges had to be built so that the packhorses and their heavy loads could cross safely. The bridges needed to be only the width of the horse, so the bridges were narrow with low parapets that allowed clearance of the loads held in panniers slung on wooden frames on either side of the horse.

The heyday of packhorse routes in the Peak District was between the 1650s and the 1750s. The earliest Peak District packhorse bridge dates from 1664 and the latest from 1734. Packhorses could carry up to 400 lbs each, and various breeds of horse were used. The most popular was derived from a German hunter called a Jaeger, which probably gave rise to the nickname 'jagger', used to describe the packhorsemen.

Further west along Edale, in the village of Grindsbrook Booth, is a classic packhorse bridge, crossing Grinds Brook close to the Old Nag's Head pub. The Nag's Head, built in 1577, would have been a typical stopping place for passing packhorsemen and at one time it was also the village blacksmith.

Other packhorse bridges can be seen near Holme Hall in Bakewell; Milldale in Dovedale; in the Burbage Valley near Longshaw; at Three Shires Head in the Staffordshire Moorlands; at Raper Lodge and Alport in Lathkill Dale; at Bowden Bridge near Hayfield; over Goyt's Clough on the Goyt Valley; and at Slippery Stones in the Upper Derwent Valley.

There is also a Jagger's Clough on the eastern slopes of Kinder Scout, first recorded as Jagger's Gate in 1688. This two-mile-long clough between Nether Moor and Crookstone Hill was formerly used by jaggers taking lead from the mines in Castleton.

Address Below the Old Nag's Head, Grindsbrook Booth, Edale, S33 7ZD, +44 (0) 1433 670291 | Getting there The Edale packhorse bridge can be found just down the lane beside The Old Nag's Head in Edale | Hours Accessible 24 hours | Tip You can follow in the footsteps of the jaggers by enjoying a pint at the Old Nag's Head in the centre of Grindsbrook Booth, Edale village. It's a traditional, stone-floored village pub, popular with walkers and famous as the starting point of the 268-mile Pennine Way.

33 Padley Chapel

Martyr's memorial

In 1588, during the reign of Elizabeth I and in the year of the Spanish Armada, the persecution of Roman Catholics, or 'recusants' as they were known, was rife. And the staunch Catholic family of the Fitzherberts of Padley Hall, at the foot of Padley Gorge near Grindleford, were high on the list of possible recusants, accused of hiding illegal priests who regularly brought the sacrament to family members and their supporters.

As a result, the hall was regularly raided by government troops and the raid that took place in July 1588 found two Catholic priests, Nicholas Garlick and Robert Ludlam, probably hiding in 'priest holes' built into the walls of the house. Having been ordained overseas, the two were charged with high treason, tried and found guilty, and two weeks later were hanged, drawn and quartered on St Mary's Bridge in Derby. Tradition has it that Garlick's head was buried in the graveyard of St John the Baptist in Tideswell, but this has never been proved. The Fitzherbert family were subsequently persecuted themselves, and John Fitzherbert died in the Tower of London in 1590. Garlick and Ludlam later became immortalised as the Padley Martyrs.

Only the grassy foundations of the courtyard of Sir Richard Fitzherbert's 14th-century Padley Hall remain today, but what was probably originally the central gatehouse survives; in 1933 it was converted from a barn (a dovecote remains in its gable end) into a Catholic chapel in honour of the martyrs, and mass was held on the premises after a break of 345 years.

Padley had been a place of pilgrimage since 1892 when the first pilgrimage took place in honour of the men who were martyred for their Catholic faith. The pilgrimages continue every July to this day, centred on the evocative remains of the chapel, and are jointly held with the Dioceses of Nottingham and Hallam.

Address Padley Chapel, Grindleford, S32 2JA, +44 (0) 1433 620989 | Getting there Park on the roadside at Grindleford Station on the B6521 Grindleford to Longshaw road and walk the 400 yards along the unmade road to reach the chapel | Hours Viewable from the outside only | Tip Longshaw Lodge, just up the road from Grindleford (+44 (0) 1433 631757), is a former shooting lodge built for the Duke of Rutland but is now owned and run by the National Trust with a popular visitor centre and café.

34 Padley Gorge

A fairytale woodland

Padley Gorge, above Grindleford, is a mile-long fairytale woodland ravine of moss and lichen-encrusted sessile oaks, beeches and silver birches, famous for its rich and rare wildlife. And most notable among this is the dainty little summer visitor, the pied flycatcher.

This mercurial migrant, which gets its name from the male's dashing black and white plumage, arrives in April and leaves in September. But when it's here for that brief nesting season, it finds the insect life supported by the mature trees, the microclimate of the gorge of the babbling Burbage Brook and the abundant nesting opportunities presented by the trunks of the gnarled and twisted old trees, ideal for raising its brood of five to eight pale blue eggs.

They're locally known as 'flickers' by birders because of their endearing habit of flicking their tails or one or both wings when they are alarmed. The pied flycatchers of Padley Gorge are a national rarity on the eastern limit of their range in Britain and bring the woodlands of Padley Gorge to life every spring with their piercing 'tzit, tzit, trui, trui' call.

These tiny birds – they are slightly smaller than a house sparrow – have made the perilous journey of over 3,000 miles, all the way from sub-Saharan Africa to reach their nesting sites in Padley Gorge. And they have been encouraged by the provision of scores of nest boxes by the landowners, the National Trust.

Padley Gorge, on the eastern edge of the Peak District National Park and on the border between Derbyshire and South Yorkshire, is a designated Site of Special Scientific Interest (SSSI). This was recognised in 1972 as being the best example of the remnant oak-birch woodland in the gritstone uplands of the Peak District.

Odd as it may seem today, Padley was also once the scene of industry, as the moss and leaf-covered abandoned remains of millstones lying among the tangled roots of the sessile oaks testify.

Address Padley Gorge, Grindleford, S32 2JA, what3words: slip.frosted.indoor | Getting there Park your car on the roadside on the B6521 Grindleford to Longshaw road and pass through the stile to reach the top end of the gorge | Hours Accessible 24 hours | Tip The nearby Grindleford Station Café (+44 (0) 1433 631011) is a bit of a legend among greasy spoon aficionados. Opened by Phil Eastwood in 1973, it retains Phil's rebellious spirit and offers the best fried food menu in the Peak.

35 Robin Hood's Stride

Where Robin strode

Robin Hood is a constant and still popular figure in English folklore and for Hollywood filmmakers, but historians have argued for years whether he actually existed or was some kind of universal medieval superhero.

Robin Hood's Stride or Mock Beggar's Hall, two natural gritstone pinnacles rising from a rocky tor near Elton, is one of several natural features in the Peak attributed to the hero's supposed superpowers. Standing 22 yards apart, the two pinnacles are said to be the length of Robin Hood's stride. They are named the Weasel, at the eastern end, and the Inaccessible to the west. The alternative name of Mock Beggar's Hall relates to their similarity to a ruined mansion when viewed from a distance.

Formed as an outlier of more resistant millstone grit in the surrounding limestone White Peak, Robin Hood's Stride is a popular place for embryo rock climbers, the two pinnacles being rated only Difficult in the climbers' scale. It's also a very popular place for amateur scramblers and for picnics for local families, who feast on the luscious bilberries that adorn its slopes.

There's also a cave in the rocks, which may be where the outlaw hid from the Sheriff of Nottingham, if the legends of the hooded adventurer are to be believed.

The rocky outcrop is a feature in an ancient landscape, a landmark on the ancient – possibly prehistoric or Roman – road known as the Derbyshire Portway (which is also known as Old Manchester Lane and The Chariot Way), and is close to the Nine Stones stone circle, which dates from the Bronze Age.

Robin Hood's Stride has featured as a scenic backdrop on the small and big screen, most notably in an episode of the TV show *The Return of Sherlock Holmes* in 1986 and the 1987 film *The Princess Bride* starring Robin Wright and Cary Elwes.

Address Robin Hood's Stride, Elton, DE4 2LZ | Getting there Robin Hood's Stride is off the B5056 Bakewell to Winster road, three miles south of Bakewell; limited parking opposite a wide farm entrance | Hours Accessible 24 hours | Tip Close by is Cratcliffe Tor, with its Hermit's Cave and the impressive Bronze Age Nine (but now only four) Stones stone circle.

36 Rowsley Station

A station without a line

When the engineers of the proposed London to Manchester Midland Line reached Rowsley at the edge of the Peak District in the 1860s, they faced a dilemma.

The easiest and most practical route would be to follow the valley of the River Derwent through the 8th Duke of Devonshire's extensive Chatsworth estate. But the Duke would not countenance a railway ploughing through his Capability Brown deer park, so an alternative route had to be planned. The next obvious route would follow the valley of the River Wye via Bakewell to Buxton.

But the Duke's neighbouring aristocrat, the Duke of Rutland, was equally opposed to a railway running through his land at Haddon Hall. The answer was to construct a 1,058-yard-long, shallow 'cut and cover' tunnel through the Haddon parkland. This was dangerous work, and in 1861 part of the tunnel collapsed and four men were killed.

Not content with putting the railway engineers to so much more expense and trouble, the two dukes also insisted that they could not use the same station as their neighbours and should have their own personal stations when they used the line. So the Midland employed architect Joseph Paxton to design and build separate stations for the Duke of Devonshire at Hassop and for the Duke of Rutland at Bakewell.

When the Midland Line finally closed in 1967, the original Rowsley Station building, designed by Paxton and dating from 1849, was retained. It now forms the centrepiece of the Peak Shopping Village. Currently housing a charity shop, it has preserved the station's arched windows and doors and projecting roof, forming a bracketed canopy round the elegant single storey building.

The station is decorated in the distinctive Chatsworth peacock blue, and the Chatsworth Kitchen on the site serves food from the estate.

Address Peak Village, Chatsworth Road, Rowsley, DE4 2JE, +44 (0) 1246 565311, www.peakrail.co.uk | Getting there From Bakewell take the A6 south, then the B6012 to Rowsley | Hours Check website for operating calendar; tearoom Wed–Sun 8.30am–3.30pm (8.30am–4.30pm on train running days) | Tip Enjoy the nostalgic thrill of travelling on a steam locomotive by taking a trip on Peak Rail (Harrison Way, Darley Dale, +44 (0) 1629 735318), which opened in 1997 and operates from the former locomotive depot at Rowsley South Station.

37 Rowtor Rocks

'A weird and wonderful place'

Tree-shrouded Rowtor Rocks has been described as 'a weird and wonderful place'. This gritstone tor is remarkable for its tunnels and caves, some of which are natural and some manmade. The series of steps, rooms, armchairs and altars date from the 18th century and were the work of the Rev Thomas Eyre, local landowner and parson of the village, who lived at Rowtor Hall.

In addition to being a priest, Eyre was also reputedly a Druid, and is said to have practised witchcraft. It is believed he used Rowtor Rocks for Druid ceremonies and wrote his sermons sitting on the seats he had carved, overlooking the landscape. Two of the caves were reputedly created by Eyre in which to entertain his Druidical friends.

Evidence that Rowtor Rocks have long held a ritual significance comes from a number of prehistoric cup and ring marks discovered at the western end of the outcrop, including a circle divided into quarters, each with a small cup and surrounded by a rosette. A short distance away is a badly eroded carving of a wavy line and associated cups, which it has been suggested might represent a serpent.

At the eastern end of the ridge there used to be a large rocking stone, weighing an estimated 50 tons, which could be rocked by hand. That was until Whit Sunday 1799, when a gang of 14 local lads pushed the stone off its balancing pivot. The stone was replaced but the essential pivot could not be restored.

In around 1700, Thomas Eyre also built a private chapel below Rowtor Rocks, which still survives and now serves as the parish church of St Michael. St Michael's was rebuilt in 1864 and is unusual in that there are windows only on two sides, the south and the east. The three two-light windows to the south side have beautiful stained glass designed by the acclaimed artist Brian Clarke in 1977, who donated them to the church when he lived at Rowtor Hall.

Address Rowtor Rocks, Main Street, Birchover, Matlock, DE4 2BL | **Getting there** Birchover is off the B5056 between Rowsley and Winster | **Hours** Accessible 24 hours | **Tip** The Red Lion Inn in Birchover's Main Street (DE4 2BN, +44 (0) 1629 650363) is a welcoming, originally 17th-century alehouse which has its own brewery, producing its own range of unique ales.

38 The Snake Pass

First to close, last to reopen

When a snowy winter descends on the Peak District, local people often judge the severity of the weather by the respective condition of two animals, the Snake and the Cat.

They are the local nicknames of the two highest cross-Pennine roads in the district: the Snake Pass carries the A57 between Sheffield and Glossop, and the Cat and Fiddle road takes the A537 between Buxton and Macclesfield.

Both roads take their names from former inns located there, which provided vital shelter and sustenance for travellers crossing the bleak and inhospitable moors on these lofty routes.

The Cat and Fiddle Inn, standing at 1,689 feet, was the second highest pub in England (the Tan Hill Inn above Reeth in Yorkshire beat it, at 1,732 feet). The Cat and Fiddle Inn closed in 2015 but reopened in 2020 as a gin and whisky distillery, shop and bar.

But the Snake Pass, which reaches 1,680 feet above sea level at Featherbed Moss between Kinder Scout and Bleaklow, is the more notorious of the two, and is often mentioned in national weather forecasts on the BBC. Due to overhanging cornices when the snow sets in, it's usually the first to be closed and the last to be reopened, and the road is frequently subject to subsidence. But in July 2025, the Department of Transport announced £7.6 million in improvements to the Snake Pass, including stabilisation of the road, speed limit signage, improved visibility and a dedicated motorcycle barrier. The winding road is a favourite route for motorcyclists.

The Snake Inn was built at the time of the opening of the turnpike road from Sheffield to Glossop in 1821. The building, now a private house, bears the date under the serpent crest of the Dukes of Devonshire over the door, from which both the road and the inn took their names.

Address Snake Pass, Bamford, S33 0BJ | Getting there The Snake Pass is on the A57 between Sheffield and Glossop, about 10 miles from Ashopton | Hours Accessible 24 hours | Tip Higher Shelf Stones, north of Snake summit, was the scene of a tragic aircraft crash in 1948. A USAF B-29 Superfortress, codenamed 'Over Exposed', crashed near the Higher Shelf Stones summit, killing all 13 crew members.

39 St Anne's Church, Baslow

'Clock' this unusual commemoration at Baslow

If you take a close look at the clock face on the east wall of the tower of St Anne's Parish Church in Baslow, you'll notice it doesn't have the usual numbers. Instead, it has the letters and date 'V I C T O R I A 1 8 9 7'. The clock on the north wall has the usual Roman numerals.

While most villages and towns chose to mark the Diamond Jubilee of Queen Victoria with memorial fountains or towers, prominent local resident Dr Edward Mason Wrench (1833–1912) decided that the 60th anniversary of the queen's accession to the throne should be commemorated with this unique horological tribute.

Although St Anne's originally dates from the 13th century, it has been subject to a number of heavy Victorian restorations, notably by Sir Joseph Paxton of nearby Chatsworth in 1852, when a new chancel was added. See if you can spot the framed whip that was formerly used by the parish dog whipper to clear the church of dogs during services – or maybe to wake up parishioners who fell asleep during the vicar's sermon!

Baslow lies below Baslow Edge on the River Derwent at the northern edge of Chatsworth Park and is still very much an estate village. Clustered around the pretty village green, which is known as Goose Green and which is bright with nodding daffodils in springtime, Baslow has five 'Ends' – Far End, Nether End, Bridge End, West End and Over End. Goose Green is at Nether End, where an ancient packhorse bridge leads through the park to Chatsworth House past a pair of thatched cottages – a rare sight in the Peak District. Bridge End is home to a 17th-century bridge over the Derwent and sports a tiny, very cramped, stone-built toll house with an entrance only 3.5 feet high. Maybe it was to collect tolls from short people only!

Address St Anne's Church, Church Street, Baslow, DE45 1RY, +44 (0) 1433 630930 | Getting there Baslow is on the A619 Chesterfield to Bakewell road | Hours Daily during daylight hours | Tip If you're feeling flush and fancy a gourmet meal, Fischers at Baslow Hall, on Calver Road, Baslow (+44 (0) 1246 583259) has an award-winning restaurant in a luxury boutique country house hotel.

40 St Mary the Virgin Church

'... among the most evocative images of Dark Age art'

St Mary the Virgin Parish Church at Wirksworth stands like a mini cathedral within its own close surrounded by gritstone town houses. For a place with a population of fewer than 5,000, it may seem a little grandiose, but St Mary's is one of the most important churches in the Peak for its wonderful collection of Anglo-Saxon carvings.

The present, heavily restored Perpendicular building dates mainly from the 13th to 15th centuries, but those Saxon monuments suggest a church has stood on this hallowed site for over a millennium, at least since the 8th century.

In 1820, a large Anglo-Saxon coffin (or sarcophagus) lid was discovered under the chancel floor. Now mounted under a window on the north wall of the nave, it appears to date from the second half of the 7th century. The richly sculptured stone slab is adorned with scenes and figures from the Bible, most of which depict the life of Christ. Simon Jenkins described it as 'one of the finest Saxon coffin lids extant' and 'among the most evocative images of Dark Age art' in his *England's Thousand Best Churches* (1999).

The church is also noted for an 8th-century Anglo-Saxon carving of a lead miner, known colloquially as 'T'owd (the old) Man', which is said to be the oldest representation of a miner anywhere in the world. It shows what appears to be a kilted miner carrying a 'wisket' (wooden basket) for his lead ore. It was moved here in 1863 for safe keeping from St James, Bonsall, but has never been returned.

The church also contains numerous other medieval carvings and fragments of larger pieces that have been grouped together and inserted in the transept walls. These include fragments of early medieval stone crosses, medieval grave slabs, figures of a wise man and shepherd, and the face of a bearded man.

Address St Mary the Virgin, St Mary's Gate, Coldwell Street, Wirksworth, DE4 4DQ, www.wirksworthteamministry.co.uk | Getting there St Mary's is in the centre of Wirksworth, reached via the B5023 from Cromford | Hours See website for details | Tip Richard Barrett's Bookshop, just off Wirksworth's sloping Market Place, is one of the finest independent second-hand bookshops in the Peak. You can browse to your heart's content among Richard's comprehensive collection of used books.

41 Stanage Edge, Hathersage

Spiders and eagles

Stanage Edge spreads like the brooding curtain wall of a medieval castle for three miles above the moors above the village of Hathersage. But its gritstone crags are a mecca for British rock climbers.

More than 850 routes, ranging from moderate to aid-assisted and highly technical, have been established on its beetling crags, which rise to 80 feet at their highest point. On a busy summer weekend, Stanage can be festooned with climbers, dangling like multi-coloured spiders on their ropes, with hang-gliders soaring like eagles above them.

The first climbers to explore these tempting, abrasive, but crack-filled faces were local climbers from Sheffield, such as J. W. Puttrell – manager of the famous cutlery company of Mappin and Webb – Lehmann Oppenheimer and E. A. Baker. With his climbing colleagues, Puttrell first explored Stanage in 1890, making the first ascents of routes using the natural lines of weakness in the faces.

But the real explosion in the exploration of Stanage and so many other Peak District crags came in the 1950s, when working-class Manchester climbers such as Joe Brown and Don Whillans laid siege to any likely looking crags. The legend that they used their mothers' washing lines for rope protection is unlikely, but now part of climbing folklore.

They established formidable routes that pushed the standards of rock climbing to new levels of difficulty, and which still challenge modern climbers today. These included the contradictory 'Right Unconquerable', the appropriately named Dangler, and Quietus at High Neb, which is close to the highest point of Stanage Edge at 1,502 feet.

Partly concealed by heather running along the edge of Stanage is a series of numbered circular basins carved out of the native gritstone. These have puzzled walkers and climbers for years but were provided as drinking holes for red grouse, which used to be managed for shooting on these moors.

Address Hollin Bank National Park car park, Stanage Edge, Hathersage, S32 1BR | Getting there On a minor road off the Ringinglow Road between Sheffield and Hathersage | Hours Accessible 24 hours | Tip The Long Causeway is the name given to the only walkable breach in the wall of Stanage Edge. It was a medieval packhorse route between the Hope Valley and Sheffield.

42 Stone Edge Chimney

The oldest industrial chimney

Standing proudly on what was once open moorland, the Stone Edge chimney near Stanage takes its place in the *Guinness World Records* as the oldest free-standing industrial chimney in Britain.

Forming part of what was once the Stone Edge lead mining cupola and dating from 1770, the four-square chimney still stands to its full height of 55 feet. It provides further evidence of the once-important lead mining industry of the Peak District during the 18th and 19th centuries, as can be also seen at Magpie Mine.

This open, exposed and barren site was chosen for the cupola – a reverberatory furnace used for smelting lead ore – because the process gave off poisonous fumes affecting vegetation, water courses and livestock. The two roads to the site are still known today as Lead Lane and Belland Lane, 'belland' being the name for the highly poisonous, finely powdered waste lead ore. Animals grazing on land contaminated with this noxious substance were said to be 'bellanded'. In 1848, the owner was involved in a legal dispute over the 'bellanding' of a horse.

The site was also chosen because of its proximity to Chesterfield – which was on the canal system and then an important market for lead; to the coal mines at Walton for the coal needed for the furnace; and to a nearby source of refractory – or fire – clay that was used to line the furnace. And of course, plentiful supplies of lead ore (galena) came from the extensive mines in the nearby limestone country of the White Peak.

Interestingly, the cupola was worked at one time by a Cornishman named Pasco who married a Sheldon girl. He was presumably one of the Cornish miners from Magpie Mine.

But by about 1860, the lead industry was in serious decline and the cupola ceased working. The ancient chimney was carefully restored by the Peak District Mines Historical Society in 1979.

Address Belland Lane, Spitewinter, Ashover, S45 OLW | Getting there Near the junction of the A632 Matlock to Chesterfield road and the B5057 from Darley Dale is Belland Lane; a footpath leads to the site | Hours Viewable 24 hours | Tip The Highfield House Farm Shop (+44 (0) 1246 590817), run by the Prince family, is just down the road from the chimney site and has a restaurant that offers wholesome, locally sourced food.

43 Strines Road

The turnpike that failed

The 12-mile Strines Road, which weaves across the Bradfield Moors in the north-east of the Peak District, is one of the most isolated, testing and scenic roads in the region. It negotiates a series of hair-raising switchbacks and hairpin bends as it dips in and out of the steep-sided cloughs that drain off the high moorland to the west.

The name comes from the Middle English meaning 'stream' or 'watercourse', but it is also known as the Mortimer Road and 'the turnpike that failed'.

The Mortimer Road turnpike, which the modern road closely follows, took its name from Hans Winthrop Mortimer (1734–1807), a landowning lawyer who was MP for Shaftesbury and Lord of the Manor of Bamford in the late 18th century. He instigated the private Act of Parliament passed in 1771 for improving the packhorse route formerly known as Halifax Gate. This led from Penistone joining the existing turnpike road between Hope and Sheffield near Mytham Bridge, and eventually on to Grindleford.

Mortimer's apparent intention was to extend it even further at either end all the way to Halifax and Matlock, and trustees of the proposed new turnpike, estimated to cost £4,056, included Lord Melbourne and the Cavendish family, Dukes of Devonshire.

But construction of the 20-mile road was delayed, and some sections were still being built in 1776. The trust was given the right to erect three turnpikes, with toll houses, now all demolished, for the turnpike. However, the turnpike was evidently not a success as it failed to attract traffic, and Mortimer died bankrupt in 1807.

The modern minor road crosses the heather moorland of Strines Moor and Broomhead Moor before crossing the mysterious earthwork known as the Bar Dyke. It then descends steeply to Ewden Bridge to reach Midhopestones and crosses the embankment of Langsett Reservoir to join the A616 Sheffield road.

Address Mortimer Road, Bradfield Dale, Sheffield, S6 6JE | **Getting there** Signposted off the A57 Sheffield to Glossop road at Moscar, about two miles east of Ladybower | **Hours** Accessible 24 hours | **Tip** Originally a manor house built in 1275, the Strines Inn (+44 (0) 114 2851247), a traditional country pub with open fires, was converted to an inn on the new turnpike in 1771.

44 Tip's Memorial

A faithful companion in life and death

When the veteran shepherd 85-year-old Joseph Tagg set out on a freezing December morning in 1953 to check on some sheep in the Upper Derwent Valley, his niece, with whom he lived at Yorkshire Bridge, wasn't unduly concerned. 'Old Joe', as he was known, knew the moors like the back of his hand and enjoyed wandering the moors with Tip, his faithful companion sheepdog, at his side.

But as darkness fell and the pair failed to return, she started to get worried and next morning she raised the alarm. Search parties were sent out to comb the area and an RAF mountain rescue team was joined by gamekeepers and fellow shepherds searching the moors. At the weekend, ramblers joined in the hunt as news of the disappearance of Old Joe and Tip began to spread.

Weeks passed and not a trace of them was found. All hope of finding Old Joe alive ceased as snow continued to fall in one of the bitterest winters ever recorded in Derbyshire, and eventually, all searches were called off.

But 15 weeks to the day after Old Joe's disappearance, two Water Board employees were rounding up some sheep high on Ronksley Moor when they came across the frozen corpse of Old Joe, lying in a grough. By his side was the emaciated Tip, who had faithfully stayed by the body of his master for an incredible 105 days.

Although she did not want to leave her master, she was taken back home by Joe's niece, nursed back to health and later awarded the Bronze Medal of the Canine Defence League, equivalent to the Victoria Cross in the animal world. Tip eventually passed away in February 1955.

Tip's story touched so many people that a public subscription was started to raise a memorial to her. Contributions came in from all parts of the world, and several months later this poignant memorial stone was unveiled by the side of the Derwent Dam.

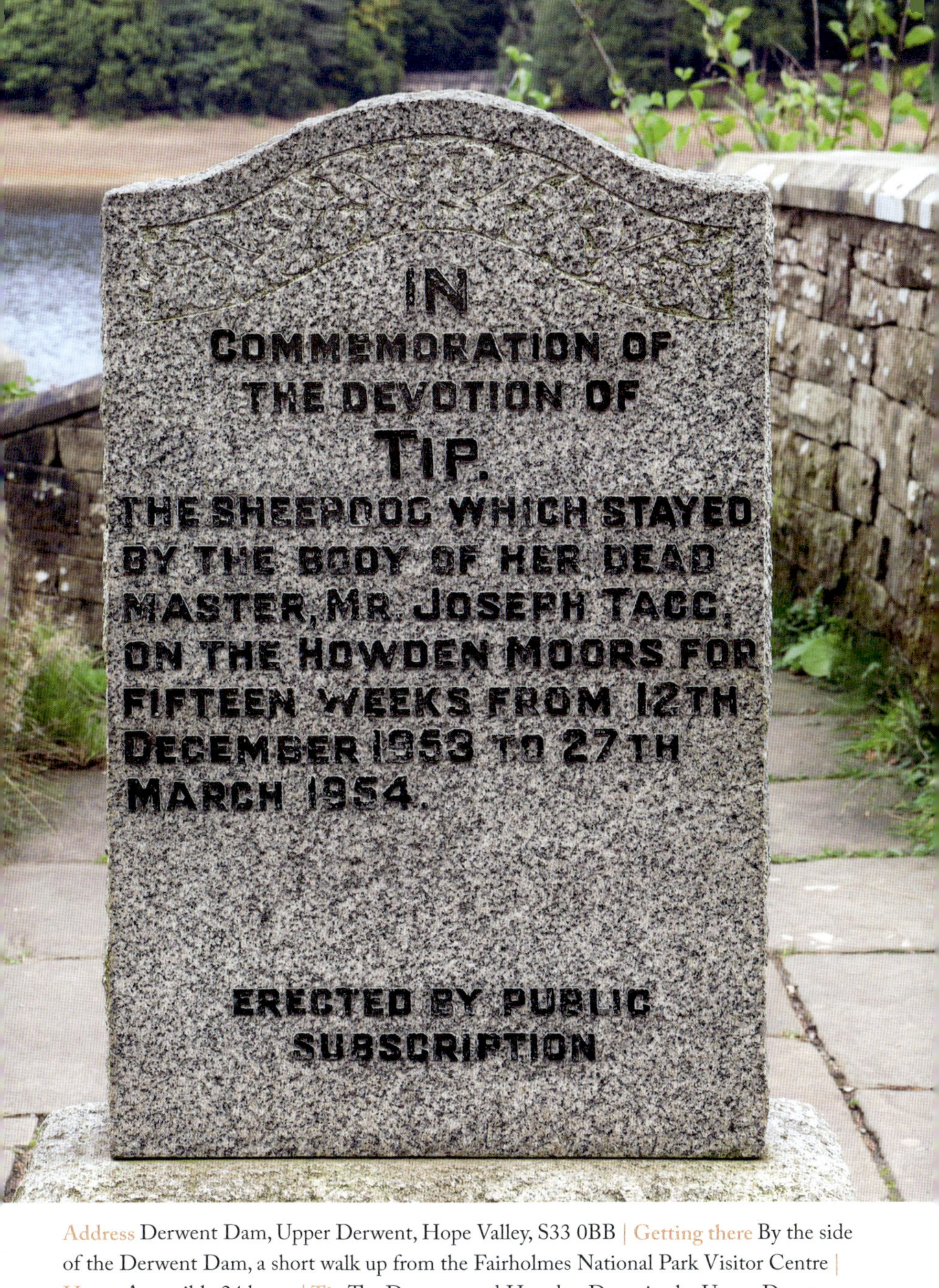

Address Derwent Dam, Upper Derwent, Hope Valley, S33 0BB | Getting there By the side of the Derwent Dam, a short walk up from the Fairholmes National Park Visitor Centre | Hours Accessible 24 hours | Tip The Derwent and Howden Dams in the Upper Derwent Valley were the scene of practice runs by the famous 'Dambuster' Lancaster bombers of 617 Squadron before their momentous raid on the Ruhr dams in 1943. There's a memorial to them inside the tower of the Derwent Dam.

45 Totley Tunnel

Tunnel vision at Totley

One of the unforgettable moments on the Sheffield to Manchester railway line is when your train bursts from the depths of the Totley Tunnel into the spectacular landscape of the Hope Valley at Grindleford.

At the time it was built in 1893, the Totley Tunnel, at three and a half miles long, was the second longest railway tunnel in the UK – only the Severn Tunnel under the Bristol Channel was longer. It is still the fourth longest on the system.

The tunnel was constructed by the Midland Railway between 1888 and 1893; the engineers were Parry and Storey of Nottingham and the contractor for 10.5 miles of the railway, including the tunnel, was Thomas Oliver of Horsham, West Sussex.

The idea was that four vertical shafts would be sunk across the moorland, and the tunnel excavated out from them. But problems beset the project from the start, because the Duke of Rutland, the major landowner, insisted that no more than one ventilation shaft should be sunk through his land and that work should cease from August to October, during the grouse shooting season.

And when work finally began in 1888, the underground conditions were found to be anything but easy. When the initial shafts were sunk through shale near the Totley end, water was encountered in the first eight feet, and alternate beds of gritstone, ganister and coal were found when the permanent shafts were sunk.

The situation was little better at the Grindleford end, where more flooding happened, and work stopped for several weeks while a drain was laid. Incredibly, a raft had to be used to inspect the workings.

Because of the damp and unhealthy underground conditions, the workforce suffered serious outbreaks of typhoid, diphtheria, smallpox and scarlet fever. Accommodation was primitive, and the workers often lived 30 to a house.

Address Station Approach, Grindleford, Hope Valley, S32 2JA | **Getting there** Just off the B6521 about a mile from Grindleford village | **Hours** Accessible 24 hours | **Tip** If you want a no-nonsense, chips-with-everything café meal, then the Grindleford Station Café (+44 (0) 1433 631011), which overlooks the western portal of the Totley Tunnel and was formerly the station house, is ideally placed. It was run by the idiosyncratic and outspoken Phil Eastwood for over 40 years.

46 Trespass Plaque

Trespassers will be celebrated

The Peak District National Park's car park in the former quarry at Bowden Bridge, Hayfield was the scene on a bright Sunday morning in April 1932 of a historic meeting, now marked by a modest bronze plaque in the quarry face.

About 400 ramblers gathered here in advance of a much-mythologised mass trespass on the then-forbidden moorland of Kinder Scout, at 2,088 feet the highest point in the Peak District. It was an event that has been described as the most important example of direct civil action in British history.

The ramblers were addressed by Benny Rothman, one of the organisers of the event, who told the khaki-clad ramblers that it was time to claim back the moorland which for centuries had been common land over which anyone could walk. That right had been stolen by the various Enclosure Acts of the 18th and 19th centuries, and now walkers were faced with misleading 'Trespassers will be Prosecuted' signs and stick-wielding gamekeepers. Not one footpath then crossed the 15-square-mile plateau of Kinder Scout.

The rest of the story is now firmly engraved in walking folklore. The ramblers set off from Bowden Bridge along a long-established right-of-way that took them into William Clough where, at a pre-arranged signal, they deliberately trespassed onto the slopes of Sandy Heys, a western outlier of Kinder Scout. There they met a group of 20 to 30 gamekeepers and after a few undignified scuffles, they continued on to meet up with a fellow group of trespassers from Edale.

When they returned triumphant to Hayfield, six of the trespassers were arrested and later five were convicted of public order (*not* trespass) offences and imprisoned for periods of between two and six months. The severity of the sentences united the rambling movement and eventually led to the Countryside and Rights of Way Act of 2000, which finally opened up those once-forbidden moorlands.

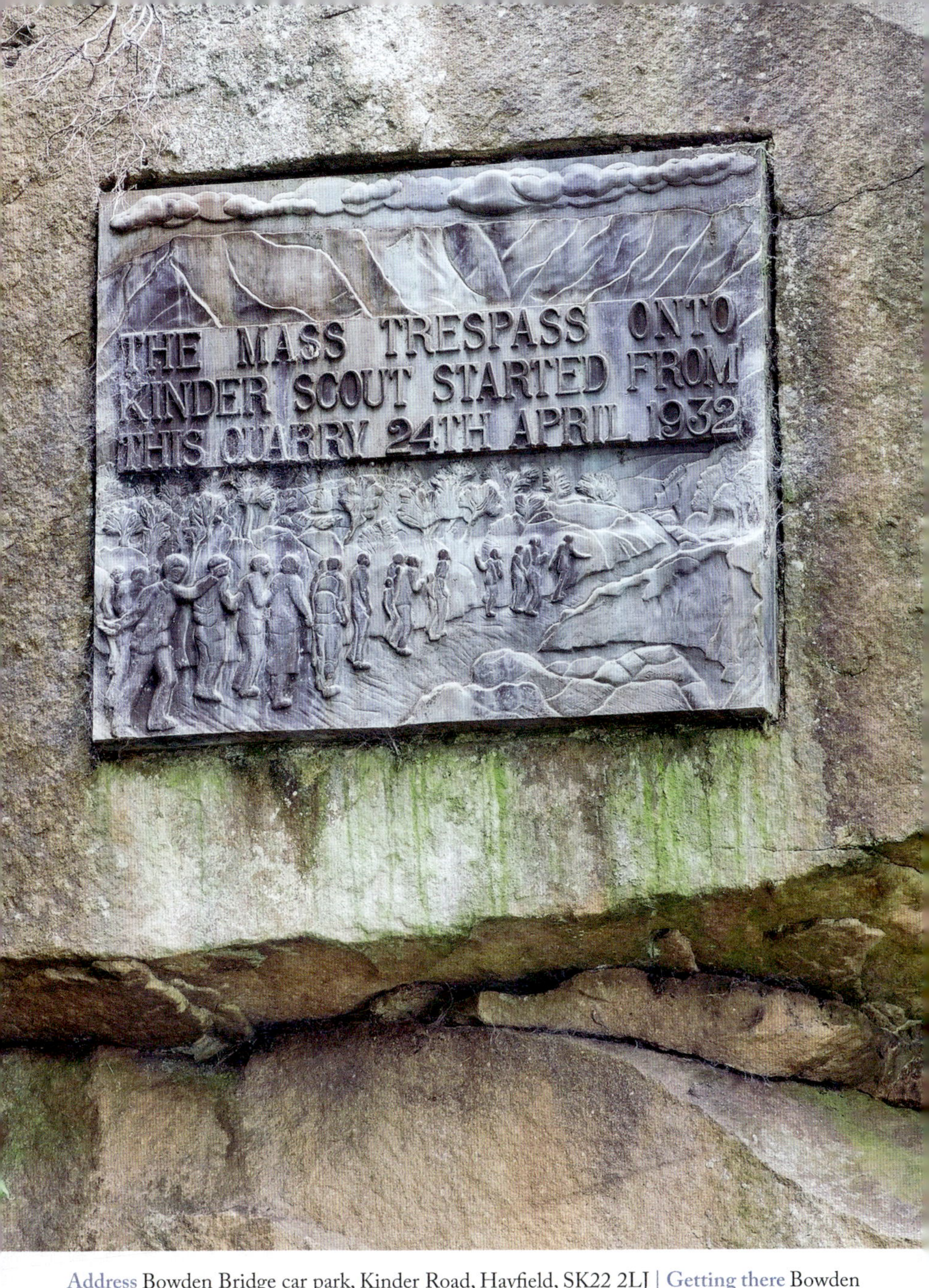

Address Bowden Bridge car park, Kinder Road, Hayfield, SK22 2LJ | Getting there Bowden Bridge quarry is about a mile east of Hayfield on Kinder Road | Hours Accessible 24 hours | Tip The Mass Trespass is recalled annually around 15 April by a celebratory event held in Hayfield, at which prominent access campaigners pay tribute to the trespassers of 1932.

47 Windgather Rocks

The friendly crag

According to a popular UK rock-climbing guide, Windgather Rocks (1,365 feet) on the Derbyshire–Cheshire border is one of the friendliest and most popular climbing crags in the Peak District. 'The tasty grades and abundance of holds on most routes mean that most people will be able to climb something here, no matter how tall, short, young, old or unfit they are,' says UKclimbing.com.

As the name implies, this west-facing crag is exposed to the prevailing westerly winds, but this also means that the rock face is generally free from vegetation and also helps it dry out quickly after rain. The guide concludes: 'Windgather is at its most delightful on warm summer evenings when the setting can be enjoyed to the full.'

The rocks lie above Taxal Edge and are part of a north-south ridge that starts between Kettleshulme and Whaley Bridge and culminates at Shining Tor, at 1,834 feet the highest point of Cheshire. Views from the top extend westwards across the Cheshire Plain towards the distant Mersey, and closer at hand towards Shining Tor.

Due to the unusual nature of the outcrop, Windgather Rocks has been designated as a Regionally Important Geological Site (RIGS). Formed during the Carboniferous period some 350 million years ago, the site that was to become Windgather Rocks then lay on the Equator and the rocks were laid down where an ancient river once met the sea in a huge delta, much like that seen with the Mississippi today.

This remains a popular site for embryo students learning the rudiments of rock climbing. The British Mountaineering Council (BMC) states that this 'beginners' crag' is 'good for teaching small children how to climb'. Most of the 50 named routes range between 'Difficult' to 'Severe' in rock climbing grades and include popular routes such as Traditional and First's Arête. A summer's evening on Windgather remains one of the joys of Peak rock climbing.

Address Near Kettleshulme, SK23 7QU | Getting there Situated above the minor road leading south from the B5470 on the western edge of Kettleshulme; limited parking by the road below the crag, and access via a fenced track | Hours Accessible 24 hours | Tip The Swan Inn (+44 (0) 1663 732943) on the Macclesfield Road at nearby Kettleshulme is an 18th-century coaching inn that specialises in delicious seafood.

48 Winking Man

Wink and you'll miss him!

The Roaches, Hen Cloud and Ramshaw Rocks in the Staffordshire Moorlands, on the western fringe of the Peak District National Park, are a classic example of what geologists call a syncline, or downfold, in the landscape.

Centred on the commanding 1,354-foot peak of Hen Cloud, sometimes known as 'the Gibraltar of Staffordshire', the land dips away to the pinkish gritstone escarpments of The Roaches and Five Clouds to the northwest and Ramshaw Rocks to the northeast, with the low-lying Coal Measures of Goldsitch Moss in the middle. Appropriately, it has been compared to a pie dish, with the rocky ridges of The Roaches, Five Clouds and Ramshaw forming the rim and coal-bearing Goldsitch Moss the filling in the middle.

The Winking Man rock (also known as the Winking Eye), is caused by a slim rib of rock jutting out from Ramshaw Rocks to the east of The Roaches, overlooking the A53. If you know when to look, it can be seen from the Leek to Buxton road about five miles from Leek. It takes on the profile of a rugged, Desperate Dan-type face when silhouetted against the sky, and the rib is pierced by an almost circular natural hole forming the eye. To the traveller driving towards Buxton on the A53, the 'eye' appears to give a cheeky wink, as another rock passes behind it in a visual phenomenon known as 'parallax'.

Unfortunately, during the 1970s the Winking Man – affectionately known locally as 'Winky' – was the victim of senseless vandalism, when the pointed tip of his nose was broken off.

The rest of heather-clad Ramshaw Rocks also take on some equally bizarre forms, with rocks resembling a cauliflower or the fissured surface of the brain, a cricket umpire's raised finger (signifying the batsman is out) and a pagan idol. See if you can find them as you take time to wander through the rocks and thoroughly explore this fascinating area.

Address what3words: essential.launcher.marmalade | Getting there The Winking Man rock can be seen from the A53 Leek to Buxton road about five miles from Leek | Hours Viewable 24 hours | Tip Caravans, campervans and motorhomes are welcome for overnight stops at the eponymous Winking Man pub, about a mile north of Ramshaw Rocks in Buxton Road, Upper Hulme (+44 (0) 1538 300361).

49 All Saints Church

Thomas' tiny tomb

The commanding, 15th-century Perpendicular tower of All Saints Parish Church, Youlgrave, standing four-square to the winds of the Peak, dominates almost every view of the former lead mining village.

There was a Saxon church here as early as the 8th century, but the building we see today at the crossroads in the centre of the village was begun in the early 12th century. The first written record of a church comes from 1155, though the village itself was mentioned in the Domesday Book of 1086.

Here it was known as *Giolgrave*, which is probably a reference to its long history of lead mining and means 'yellow grove or groove' – a groove being an old name for a lead working. But it has been spelt in over 60 different ways since the Middle Ages, including *Jalgrave, Iolgrave, Yelgreve* and even *Hyolegrave*. Even today, there are two spellings of the name, and it goes by the local nickname of 'Pommy'.

The circular Norman font originally belonged to Elton church and has a writhing salamander (a symbol of baptism) supporting a stoup, or extension of the main bowl, carved into its support.

The impressive chancel holds two especially interesting tombs. In the middle stands a miniature three-and-a-half-foot-long alabaster effigy of a fully armoured Sir Thomas Cockayne, his hands raised in prayer – he died in 1488, allegedly after a fight over a family marriage settlement. The smaller-than-life effigy apparently indicates that he died before his father. And set against the north wall of the chancel is the weathered effigy of a bearded knight said to depict Sir John Rossington, shown tenderly holding his heart in his hands.

The beautiful stained glass east window was designed by Edward Burne-Jones and produced in the workshops of William Morris. Opposite the main door, at the end of the north aisle, is a small 12th-century carved figure thought to represent a robed pilgrim and an unusual Catholic dedication to Charles I, King and Martyr.

Address All Saints Church, Alport Road, Youlgrave, DE45 1WS | Getting there Youlgrave is on the minor road leading west off the A6 south of Bakewell | Hours Daily 9am–4pm (9am–3pm in winter) | Tip There's a choice of two excellent traditional village pubs in Youlgrave: The George Hotel, opposite the church on Alport Lane (+44 (0) 1629 636292), and the Farmyard Inn on Main Street (+44 (0) 1629 636221).

50 Arbor Low

Stonehenge of the North

Stand on the crest of the Arbor Low henge on a warm summer's day and the only sound you'll hear, apart from the soft soughing of the wind, will be the tinkling silver song of skylarks cascading from the azure sky.

It's humbling to think that the Neolithic people who built this still-impressive monument some 5,000 years ago would have heard exactly the same song and seen the same 360-degree view that you are enjoying on this airy monument, some 1,200 feet above the sea.

Arbor Low, on Middleton Common near Monyash, is the most famous and impressive prehistoric site in the Peak and is sometimes dubbed 'the Stonehenge of the North'. But for atmosphere and the feeling of closeness with the past, it far outshines its over-interpreted, now inaccessible and overcrowded counterpart on Salisbury Plain.

The Arbor Low henge and stone circle together with its attendant burial mounds were thoroughly investigated in the 19th century by pioneering local archaeologist Thomas Bateman from nearby Middleton-by-Youlgrave. But the origin and purpose of the circular earthwork and ditch with its circle of 50 fallen limestone monoliths inside remain a mystery.

Current thinking is that it must have been some kind of important sacred or ritual site for the people of the Neolithic age, who deliberately built it in a clearing in the surrounding woodland to command that wonderful panorama of the White Peak.

Archaeologists are now agreed that the massive stones of the Arbor Low circle must originally have stood upright, just like all the other stone circles in Britain. A cratered Bronze Age burial mound (the result of another Bateman dig) is superimposed on the south-eastern rim of the henge, and a couple of fields away lies the massive tumulus of Gib Hill, which consists of another Bronze Age round barrow superimposed on a Neolithic long barrow.

Address Long Rake, Monyash, Bakewell, DE45 1JS | **Getting there** Signposted from the A515 Ashbourne to Buxton Road when you turn onto the minor road to Monyash at Parsley Hay; access is through a farmyard where the owner makes a nominal charge | **Hours** Accessible during daylight hours | **Tip** Just across the A515, Parsley Hay is a former railway station and now a cycle hire centre on the popular Tissington Trail.

51 Bateman's Grave

Tomb of the Barrow Knight

Tucked away behind the former Congregational Chapel in Middleton-by-Youlgrave is the extraordinary tomb of an extraordinary man.

The stone tomb, surrounded by spear-headed cast iron railings and set on a low stone plinth, is surmounted at its west end with a replica of a Bronze Age collared cinerary urn bearing the inscription 'Thos Bateman Esq Died. Aug 28th 1861 aged 39 years'.

Known as 'the Barrow Knight' and recognised as the godfather of Peak District archaeology, Thomas Bateman, who lived at nearby Lomberdale Hall, excavated more than 200 burial mounds (or barrows) during his short but highly productive life. He and his two colleagues, Samuel Carrington of Wetton and James Ruddock of Pickering in Yorkshire, were probably responsible for opening double that number.

Bateman's two published books recording his excavations – *Vestiges of the Antiquities of Derbyshire* (1847) and *Ten Years' Diggings* (1861) – are now recognised as pioneering works from the earliest days of the emerging science of archaeology. But unusually for the time, Bateman was no mere treasure hunter, meticulously recording everything he found and setting new standards for his day, making him highly regarded by archaeologists today.

Bateman was born at Rowsley, the only son of William Bateman, heir to a prosperous cotton business with a keen interest in antiquarianism himself, digging the barrows at Arbor Low and Gib Hill.

Some of Bateman's most notable finds were the barrow at Benty Grange, which revealed the burial of a possible princely member of the Anglo-Saxon Pecsaetan tribe, complete with his boar-crested helmet (now in Sheffield's Weston Park Museum); and the Neolithic long barrow on Gib Hill, near Arbor Low, from which Bateman removed the stone-lined cist (or burial chamber) to his garden at Lomberdale Hall (it has since been returned).

Address Bateman's Grave, rear of Chapel House, Middleton-by-Youlgrave, Bakewell, DE45 1LS | Getting there Middleton-by-Youlgrave is a mile southwest of Youlgrave on a minor road that follows the north side of Bradford Dale; Bateman's tomb is behind the former chapel in Middleton (now a private house) and is accessed via a short signed footpath | Hours Accessible 24 hours | Tip It's a three-mile walk from Middleton up Long Rake to reach the scene of two of Bateman's most famous excavations at Arbor Low and Gib Hill.

52 Beresford Dale

Dovedale away from the crowds

In the busy summer holiday period, the lower reaches of the River Dove are best avoided, as its popularity can result in brimming car parks and queues at the Stepping Stones. But the upper reaches, including Beresford and Wolfscote Dales, are much less frequented, and here you can enjoy relatively peaceful walking in equally splendid and interesting scenery.

Just a short, mile-long walk from the village of Hartington, passing the possible Romano-British settlement site and strip lynchets of Pennilow, you enter the wooded confines of Beresford Dale. In the woodland to your right stands the Fishing Temple (private) built in 1674 by Charles Cotton in honour of his friend and co-author of *The Compleat Angler*, Izaak Walton.

Crossing a pretty wooden footbridge, you soon come to a tree-embowered bend in the river with a tall pinnacle of rock standing proud. This is Pike Pool, presumably named after the fish. A squeezer stile and another footbridge soon bring you to the junction of Beresford and Wolfscote Dales, and two prominent limestone crags on your left, the first housing a small cave known as Frank i' the Rock cave, about 50 feet above the river.

A hundred years ago, the antiquarian Dr L. S. Palmer explored this deep, narrow fissure in the rocks. He found the remains of at least 10 people (strangely mostly children), two bronze brooches, bronze pins, nine beads of various types, an antler cheek-piece, and other objects including Roman, Romano-British and medieval pottery. Eight Roman coins were also discovered, dating from A.D. 300–400.

The cave is thought by archaeologists to have been a burial rather than a settlement site, and animal remains found in various parts of the cave included sheep, ox, fallow deer, pig, horse, dog, badger, pine marten, polecat and hare.

Address Mill Lane, Hartington, Buxton, SK17 0AN | Getting there The junction of Beresford and Wolfscote Dales; Frank i' the Rock cave is a one-mile walk from Hartington, signposted off the B5054 Warslow road from Rookes Pottery in Mill Lane | Hours Accessible 24 hours | Tip If you are staying in the area and on a limited budget, you might try an overnight stay at Hartington Hall Youth Hostel (+44 (0) 345 371 9740), on Hall Bank, Hartington. Its previous 'hostellers' include Bonnie Prince Charlie, who is alleged to have stayed in this fine 17th-century manor house during his abortive 1745 uprising.

53 Brindley Memorial

The man who linked the seas

John Ruskin, the distinguished Victorian polymath, claimed that James Brindley, 'the Father of the English Canal System', had 'chained seas together' and that 'his ships do visibly float over valleys'. Despite being virtually illiterate, Brindley (1716–1772) was one of the most notable English civil engineers of the 18th century, and transformed England's transportation system. He built 365 miles of canals, in addition to many watermills and other machinery.

Brindley's local memorial is the triangular canopy that covers the fountain on the sunken green in the village of Wormhill, near Tunstead, also the site of one of the village's two well dressings. It carries a simple inscription: '1875. In Memory of James Brindley, canal engineer, born in this parish. AD 1716.'

Brindley was born in the tiny hamlet of Tunstead to a family of yeoman farmers. Showing no aptitude for reading and writing, he received little formal education, being largely taught at home by his mother. At the age of 17 he was apprenticed to a millwright in Sutton, near Macclesfield, where he soon showed exceptional skill and inventiveness. Brindley's growing reputation as a civil engineer brought him to the attention of the 3rd Duke of Bridgewater, who was looking for a way to transport coal from his mines at Worsley to the burgeoning industrial city of Manchester.

In 1759 the Duke commissioned Brindley as the consulting engineer for the construction of the 39-mile Bridgewater Canal, which would open in 1761. The canal, which ran between Runcorn and Leigh, is regarded as the first British canal of the modern era.

Brindley was soon commissioned to construct more canals, including the Staffordshire and Worcestershire Canal, the Oxford Canal and numerous others. He also extended the Bridgewater Canal to Runcorn, connecting it to his next major work, the Trent and Mersey Canal.

Address Wormhill, High Peak, SK17 8SL | **Getting there** Located about 1.5 miles northwest of Miller's Dale on the B6049 between the A6 and Tideswell | **Hours** Accessible 24 hours | **Tip** The Parish Church of St Margaret's has an unusual Rhenish, helmet-shaped cap to its tower, said to be a replica of the Saxon tower at Sompting in Sussex. The church was heavily restored in 1864, and the base of the tower is all that remains of the medieval church. There is also a Saxon cross in the churchyard with a sundial and an unusual pyramid-shaped tomb.

54__Buxton Opera House

The Theatre in the Hills

The singer walked onto the stage of the Buxton Opera House and gazed open-mouthed at the sumptuously painted and gilded auditorium. 'Wow,' he exclaimed. 'It's like performing inside a Fabergé egg!' It was a typical response from the many artists who have performed in the beautiful 'Theatre in the Hills' since its inception.

Frank Matcham's Art Nouveau masterpiece has attracted admirers ever since it opened in June 1903. Matcham (1854–1920) was one of the most prolific and admired theatre architects of his time, designing among many others the Palladium and Coliseum in London, and the Theatre Royal, Newcastle.

The 900-seat theatre, which cost the now seemingly modest sum of £25,000, is lavishly decorated with marble walls and stairs, glittering gilding and six romantic pastel-painted panels. The coat of arms of Buxton is displayed over the proscenium arch, flanked by winged cherubs and caryatids. The theatre was an immediate success, attracting artists of the calibre of ballerina Anna Pavlova, and actor Alec Guinness, who played a modern dress *Hamlet* in 1938. In 1927, it was turned into a cinema, showing black-and-white films.

It became the venue for an annual summer festival from 1936 to 1942, initially in conjunction with Lilian Baylis and her London-based Old Vic company. But after the Second World War, the theatre gradually fell into disrepair, and in 1976 it was closed. But in 1979, the building was restored under the auspices of a charitable trust, and an orchestra pit was added to the original Matcham design. Further restoration took place from 1999 to 2001, and in 2007 further extensive programmes of internal and external restoration took place.

Since July 1979, the Opera House has been home to the Buxton International Arts Festival, which runs for about two weeks in mid-July and has developed into one of Britain's largest opera-based festivals.

Address Buxton Opera House, Water Street, SK17 6XN, buxtonoperahouse.org.uk | **Getting there** Buxton is on the A6, A515 and A53; theatre signposted from town centre | **Hours** Viewable from the outside 24 hours; see website for performance schedule | **Tip** The Old Hall Hotel, opposite the Opera House in The Square, (+44 (0) 20 3027 6614) was originally a 16th-century fortified tower where Mary Queen of Scots stayed when taking the Buxton waters while under the custodianship of the Earl of Shrewsbury between 1573 and 1584.

55 Church of the Holy Cross

A tragic nativity

St Bertram (also sometimes called Bertelin, Beorhthelm or Bettelin) was a legendary 8th-century Anglo-Saxon saint who is said to have ended his days as a hermit at Ilam, at the southern entrance to Dovedale. His shrine – a simple tomb with open quatrefoils in the south aisle of the Church of the Holy Cross – was a popular place of pilgrimage in the Middle Ages.

Bertram's life was plagued by tragedy. The story goes he was a pious Mercian prince who travelled to Ireland to escape the wickedness of his father. There he fell in love with an Irish princess and eloped with her to England, where she became pregnant. When the birth was imminent, Bertram was away and his wife and her newborn were attacked by wolves and killed, and the heartbroken Bertram was driven into the life of a hermit.

The church, set in the Italianate gardens and parkland of Ilam Hall, holds a wonderful collection of Saxon crosses, a Norman font and some superb later memorials. Heavily restored by Sir George Gilbert Scott between 1855 and 1856, the Early English saddleback west tower and arch date from the 13th century.

The octagonal Pike-Watts Memorial Chapel was built in 1831 by Jesse Watts-Russell, a wealthy London brewer and vintner, long-time owner of the Hall and creator of the village, in honour of his father-in-law, David Pike Watts (d. 1816). It is dominated by Sir Francis Chantrey's moving and lifelike snow-white marble sculpture of Pike-Watts lying on a couch, sitting up to bless his daughter and three grandchildren.

Other memorials include the beautifully carved and painted alabaster tomb to Robert Meverell (d. 1626) and his wife. The circular Norman font illustrates episodes from the tragic life of St Bertram and there are two Anglo-Saxon crosses in the churchyard. And just to the south of the church, on Paradise Walk, is St Bertram's Well.

Address Holy Cross Church, Ilam, DE6 2AZ, www.achurchnearyou.com/church/4330 | **Getting there** On the minor road between Thorpe and Alstonefield | **Hours** See website for contact details | **Tip** Ilam is on the doorstep of Dovedale, a honeypot best avoided on a summer weekend. But if you go off season and midweek, you can sometimes enjoy Charles Cotton's 'princess of rivers' and have the famous stepping stones across the river to yourself.

56 Ecton Hill

Deepest and richest

There's not much to be seen on the surface today, but during the 18th century, Ecton Hill Copper Mine in the Manifold Valley was a hive of industry and the deepest and most productive copper mine in Britain.

It produced over 100,000 tons of copper ore, and made its owner, the 5th Duke of Devonshire, profits of over £300,000, financing, it is claimed, the building of his magnificent Crescent in Buxton.

Now run by the Ecton Mine Educational Trust, it has today become an important educational resource, which leads children into the darkest depths of Ecton's history.

We know that copper has been mined at Ecton since the Bronze Age some 3,500 years ago, after hammerstones and a radio-carbon-dated antler tool were discovered in some of the shallower workings on the hill. It was mined commercially from the early 17th to the late 19th century, but the peak period was in the second half of the 18th century, when it became one of the richest copper mines in Britain.

The copper ore from Ecton was notably richer than that obtained from other mines – recording up to 15 per cent in its purity. And gunpowder was used for the first time in a British mine at Ecton in 1670. But by the 19th century, Devon and Cornwall were producing up to half the world's supply of copper, and by the 1890s, working at Ecton had ceased.

Visible surface remains today include an early (1788) Boulton and Watt steam-powered winding engine house, some ruinous 19th-century mine buildings, fern-draped adit (horizontal shaft) entrances, gin circles and pipe entrances.

The copper-covered, bright-green-stained spire of the Gothic castle-looking folly in Ecton village is a permanent, visible reminder of the underground riches that made Ecton a wonder of the pre-industrial world.

Address Ecton Hill, Ashbourne, DE6 2AH | Getting there Ecton Hill is most easily reached from the Manifold Trail but is on the minor road between Wetton and Hulme End | Hours Accessible 24 hours | Tip The 400-year-old Royal Oak in the centre of the village of Wetton (+44 (0) 1335 310287) is a real walkers' pub a few miles from Ecton, which describes itself as a 'food hub'.

57 Eldon Hole

Gateway to Hell

About a mile north of the village of Peak Forest on the southern slopes of Eldon Hill gapes Eldon Hole, the biggest open pothole in the Peak District.

Long thought to be bottomless and the entrance to Hell, it was descended for the first time by John Lloyd, a Fellow of the Royal Society, in 1770, and found to be a mere 245 feet deep. There are apocryphal tales, repeated by Charles Cotton in his *Wonders of the Peak*, of a goose being lowered into the awesome void in Tudor times, only to emerge three days later at another wonder, Peak Cavern (or The Devil's Arse), in Castleton, with its feathers apparently singed by the fires of Hell. Cotton also claims that he let down a line 800 fathoms (4,800 feet, or about a mile) into the hole without reaching the bottom. He failed to realise that his rope might have just been coiling up at the bottom.

Cotton also tells the story of the Earl of Leicester, who was a guest at Chatsworth, persuading a servant to be lowered into the depths of Eldon Hole. He was lowered to the rope's limit of 100 yards before he was hauled out, raving mad after his apparent descent into Hell. The servant died still delirious eight days later, convincing the Earl that the realm of Hades lay in the bottom of the fearsome pit.

Today, the tree-fringed entrance and depths of Eldon Hole are strictly the preserve of expert potholers and cavers, but the drystone wall and fence that encircles it are regularly demolished and thrown into the hole, causing the occasional sheep or cow to fall into its gaping maw.

About 300 yards north of Eldon Hole is Eldon Hill, a 1,540-foot limestone summit brutally disfigured by a huge but now disused limestone quarry on its west face, which gave it the nickname of 'the worst eyesore in the Peak'. The quarry closed in 1999 and now lies within the Castleton Site of Special Scientific Interest (SSSI), as nature recovers the site.

Address Eldon Hole, Peak Forest, SK17 8EN | **Getting there** An easy two-mile walk north from Church Street in Peak Forest, which is on the A623 Baslow to Chapel-en-le-Frith road | **Hours** Accessible 24 hours | **Tip** The Parish Church of King Charles the Martyr in Peak Forest (built by the Catholic-sympathising Devonshire family) was once the Peak's Gretna Green, where couples could be married without the reading of the banns – it lay within the Royal Forest of the Peak and was thus outside church jurisdiction.

58 Eleanor Cross

A monument in memory of Mary

The Gothic-style Mary Watts-Russell Cross in the centre of the estate village of Ilam (pronounced 'Eye-lamb') is deliberately reminiscent of a medieval Eleanor Cross. Designed by Sir George Gilbert Scott, the memorial, also known as the Ilam Cross, was erected in 1841 in memory of Mary by her beloved husband, Jesse Watts-Russell of nearby Ilam Hall.

After the death of Eleanor of Castile in 1290, Edward I commissioned a series of large stone memorial crosses to his beloved wife of 18 years, to be placed at 12 sites along the route her body had been taken from Lincoln, her place of death, to Westminster Abbey, her burial place. Each of these 'Eleanor Crosses' was at least 42 feet tall and featured a representation of her likeness.

In addition to the Ilam Cross, in the 1800s Watts-Russell, the son of a wealthy soap manufacturer, began remodelling the village of Ilam. He is believed to have found Dovedale and its surrounding hills reminiscent of the Swiss Alps, and consequently built new chalet-style houses (rehousing most of the villagers) and a matching schoolhouse here. In 1857 – at a time when education was not compulsory – he also built and funded the village school, as well as the neo-Gothic Ilam Hall.

The first Ilam Hall had been built by John Port in 1546, and his family owned it for 250 years. Both the playwright William Congreve and the lexicographer Samuel Johnson stayed at the hall; Congreve wrote his first play, *The Old Bachelor*, here and the nearby Paradise Valley is supposed to have inspired Johnson to write his novel *Rasselas*.

Demolition of Ilam Hall was well advanced by the early 1930s, when Sir Robert McDougal bought it for the National Trust. This was on the condition that the remaining parts (the entrance porch and hall, the Great Hall and the service wing) be used as a youth hostel, which it remains today.

Address Ilam, Ashbourne, DE6 2AZ | Getting there The village is signposted 2.5 miles off the A515 Ashbourne to Buxton road | Hours Accessible 24 hours | Tip If you fancy a cuppa, the Manifold Tea-room at Ilam Hall (+44 (0) 1335 350245) is ideally situated with stunning views of Thorpe Cloud and the Italianate gardens of the hall.

59 The Fountain

Monument to a special lady

In the porous limestone landscape of the White Peak where water is a precious commodity, the former lead mining village of Youlgrave has a very special claim to fame. It is one of a handful of villages in Britain still entirely served by its own private water supply.

And in the centre of the village square, on the site of its ancient Saxon cross, an unusual circular, nine-foot-high stone-built monument known to villagers as The Fountain stands as proud evidence of Youlgrave's aqueous independence.

More accurately a water storage tank or conduit head, The Fountain was constructed in 1829 on the initiative of a remarkable local spinster, already then in her seventies. Hannah Bowman (1758–1842) was a daughter of a well-known local Quaker farming family, committed to doing good work for the community. In 1827, Hannah formed the Youlgrave Friendly Society of Women and promoted the idea that a constant water supply could be conveyed by pipes to the village.

The project quickly gained support, and under Hannah's guidance a subscription fund (today it would be called 'crowdfunding') was set up. Miss Bowman gave £100 herself, while a further donation of £50 came from Lord of the Manor, the Duke of Rutland. Local surveyor Benjamin Staley came up with a scheme to convey locally fed spring water through 1,100 yards of two-inch-diameter cast-iron pipes to the 1,500-gallon-capacity conduit head. The gritstone walled tank was constructed at a cost of £31 10 shillings (around £72 today) and the entire scheme was completed at a cost of £252 13 shillings and tenpence halfpenny (just under £23,000 today).

In order to run the waterworks, the Youlgrave Waterworks Company was formed and is still going strong. Since 1996 it has been a limited company run by 12 volunteer directors for the benefit of the community – which is charged less than 10p per annum per household.

Address The Fountain, The Square, Youlgrave, Bakewell, DE45 1UR | Getting there Three miles south of Bakewell off the A6 Bakewell to Matlock road | Hours Accessible 24 hours | Tip Youlgrave Youth Hostel (+44 (0) 845 371 9151), opposite The Fountain, is housed in the former Youlgrave Cooperative Store, and includes an artisan bakery and café named Fountain View. One of its claims to fame is that gentlemen can sleep in a bedroom still labelled 'Ladies Underwear'!

60 Haddon Hall

A dream castle by the Wye

Standing proud on a limestone bluff overlooking the River Wye is the impossibly romantic Haddon Hall, one of the finest medieval halls in Britain. Haddon was memorably described by architectural historian Nikolaus Pevsner as: '...the English castle par excellence, not the forbidding fortress on an unassailable crag, but the large, rambling, safe, grey, lovable house of knights and their ladies, the unreasonable dream-castle of those who think of the Middle Ages as a time of chivalry and valour and noble feelings'.

The hall is the Derbyshire home of Lord and Lady Edward Manners, but it owes its marvellous state of almost complete medieval preservation to the fact that it stood empty and neglected for over 200 years. The Manners family chose Belvoir Castle in Leicestershire as their main home in 1703, which meant that Haddon stood frozen in time until it was occupied again in the early 20th century.

Such is their medieval perfection, that Haddon's embattled courtyard and rose-entwined walls have become a common backdrop to many film and television dramas, and Pevsner's 'dream-castle' continues to be a popular film set.

The oldest part of the house is the 12th-century chapel, still adorned with beautiful though faint medieval wall paintings, including a lively representation of St Christopher carrying the Christ child on his shoulders. Haddon's chapel is still the parish church for the deserted medieval village of Nether Haddon, the remains of which, in the right light, can still be traced in the bumps and hollows across the busy buzz of the modern A6.

Everything at Haddon exudes history, from the hollowed, time-worn oak steps and basins and wonderful collection of dole cupboards in the Tudor kitchens, to the magnificent Long Gallery, whose panelling is decorated with peacocks and boars' heads, representing respectively the Manners and Vernon families.

Address Haddon Hall, Bakewell, DE45 1LA, www.haddonhall.co.uk | Getting there On the A6, two miles south of Bakewell | Hours See website for seasonal opening hours | Tip While in Bakewell, you might like to visit the parish church of All Saints, where the ornate, storied tomb of Lord John Manners and his wife Dorothy Vernon – who is alleged to have eloped with him after a ball at Haddon Hall – is a feature of the Newark Chapel.

61 Harboro Rocks

Encounter with a lead miner

Travelling through Derbyshire in his *Tour Through the Whole Island of Great Britain* in the early 18th century, Daniel Defoe, creator of *Robinson Crusoe*, came across the jagged, Dolomitic limestone outcrop known as Harboro or Brassington Rocks. Here he encountered a family of seven who 'seemed to live very pleasantly' in a cave known as the Giant's Tomb, which is now a Scheduled Ancient Monument. Archaeologists have found evidence of human occupancy in the cave dating back to the last Ice Age, and there is evidence of a Romano-British settlement and terraced field system dating from the 3rd century at nearby Rainster Rocks.

The woman in the cave told Defoe that her husband was a lead miner, and he later met 'the poor wretch' emerging from a mine in the valley below, who was 'as lean as a skeleton, pale as a dead corps [sic], his hair and beard a deep black, his flesh lank and, as we thought, something of the colour of the lead itself,' wrote Defoe. He also observed that 'being very tall and very lean he look'd like an inhabitant of the dark regions below'.

Mind you, Defoe didn't seem to have a high opinion of Peaklanders anyway, famously describing them as '…a rude boorish kind of people'. But he added that they were 'a bold, daring, and even desperate kind of fellows in their search into the bowels of the earth'.

The darker-coloured Dolomitic limestone of the Brassington area contrasts markedly with the predominant grey and white Carboniferous limestone found elsewhere in the White Peak. Affected by underground heat and compaction under extreme pressure, it formed as a magnesium replacement of limestone, before turning into the dark brown Dolomitic rock, which takes its name from the Dolomite mountain range in north-eastern Italy. It can be easily seen in the change of colour in the rocks of the locally abundant drystone walls.

Address Harboro Rocks, near Brassington, DE4 4DD | Getting there The High Peak Trail follows the south-west side of the hill, and the Limestone Way long-distance footpath passes to the north-west | Hours Viewable 24 hours | Tip Carsington Water (+44 (0) 330 678 0701), holding nearly eight billion gallons of water, is the ninth largest reservoir in England. Situated between Wirksworth and Kniveton off Big Lane, Carsington, it has shops, a restaurant, and facilities for fishing, water sports and horse riding.

62__Hartington Cheese

Say 'cheese' at Hartington

By tradition and official certification, tasty, blue-veined Stilton cheese can only be made in the neighbouring counties of Derbyshire, Leicestershire and Nottinghamshire. The original creamery at Hartington was established by the Duke of Devonshire in the 1870s and was the first to produce Derbyshire Stilton, a white, crumbly cheese. This first creamery was partially destroyed by fire in 1894.

After standing empty for six years, in 1900 it was taken over and recommissioned by Thomas Nuttall, an award-winning Stilton cheese maker from Melton Mowbray in Leicestershire. He was largely responsible for the legacy that made Nuttall's Hartington Stilton cheese famous throughout the world, and the company that bore his name continued production until 2009.

During the 1930s, an official Certification Trademark confined the legal production of Blue Stilton to the three counties, keeping the cheese special and protecting the name from copies. This was further reinforced in 2014 by Stilton being granted Protected Designation of Origin (PDO) status by the European Union. PDO is a mark of excellence that proves a product's unique characteristics depend 'essentially or exclusively' on the geographical place of its origin.

The tradition of Hartington cheese was revived in 2012, when the new Hartington Creamery made its first cheese at the historic Pikehall Farm in the hamlet of Pikehall across the A515 from Hartington. Pikehall Farm dates back to 1759, when it was a toll house on the Nottingham to Newhaven turnpike road called the Pikeham Inn. It became a farm in 1875 and the original remains of what could be a Roman road go straight through the farmyard up into the fields, where the farm's 200 dairy cows still use it as their daily highway to the milking parlour. The first products produced at the new creamery were Peakland Blue and Peakland White, both of which are still unique to Hartington.

Address Hartington Creamery, Pikehall Farm, Hartington, DE4 2PH, hartingtoncreamery.co.uk; The Old Cheese Shop, Market Place, Hartington, SK17 0AL, www.hartingtoncheeseshop.co.uk | **Getting there** About three miles from Hartington, on the A5012 off the A515 Buxton to Ashbourne road | **Hours** The creamery is not open to the public, but you can purchase their cheese from their website or from The Old Cheese Shop in Hartington (see above) | **Tip** There are a couple of fine hostelries in Hartington, both excellent places in which to down a pint after enjoying some Stilton cheese. They are the Charles Cotton (+44 (0) 1298 84229) and The Devonshire Arms (+44 (0) 1298 601154).

63 Heights of Abraham

Heights of delight

When Andrew and Vanessa Pugh first set eyes on the Heights of Abraham, which tower 450 feet above the gorge of the River Derwent at Matlock Bath, it was in a snowstorm.

The London-based couple had been looking around for a business opportunity when they came across an advertisement in 1974 for an estate with woods, caves and a house. 'We'd never been to Derbyshire before, but were intrigued,' said Andrew in a 2011 interview. 'So we set off and by the time we got there, the rain had turned to snow. Vanessa was dressed for London, and we had to park at the Lodge and walk up to the house, which was quite a challenge.'

The couple were 'absolutely speechless' by the time they reached the Prospect Tower and were so enthusiastic after they had toured the Masson and Great Rutland/Nestus Caverns and climbed the Victoria Prospect Tower that they decided to buy it.

Fifty years later, the 60-acre Heights of Abraham leisure park is the second most popular visitor attraction in the Peak District (after Chatsworth). The famous cable cars that whisk the visitor 586 yards up to the Heights were installed by the Pughs in 1984 at a cost of £1 million. They enable visitors not to have to endure the strenuous climb faced by Andrew and Vanessa, but if you are feeling fit, you can still do that by buying a pedestrian ticket at the West Lodge in Upperwood Road, Matlock Bath.

The Victoria Prospect Tower was built in 1844 to celebrate the reign of Queen Victoria. From the top of the tower there are panoramic views of the valley of the River Derwent, Matlock Bath and the nearby Riber and Willersley Castles.

The Heights of Abraham gained their name at the time of the death of General James Wolfe at the Battle of Quebec in 1759, a battle that led to Britain's acquisition of Canada under the Treaty of Paris in 1783.

Address The Heights of Abraham, Matlock Bath, DE4 3NT, +44 (0) 1629 582365, www.heightsofabraham.com | Getting there Signposted off the A6 in Matlock Bath | Hours Check website for seasonal opening times | Tip The various attractions of the Heights of Abraham park include two adventure playgrounds and the amazing 360-degree view from the spiral-staircased Victoria Prospect Tower.

64 Hope Pinfold

That sheep may safely graze

There are at least half a dozen small, stone-walled and usually empty, enclosures in the centre of Peak District villages going by the generic name of 'pinfold', which can sometimes puzzle visitors.

A pinfold is an enclosure in which stray animals were kept until the owner could retrieve them. The name is thought to have derived from the Old English *pundfald*, meaning an enclosure.

Pinfolds are known to date from the Middle Ages, and by the 16th century most villages would have had one. They still exist at places like Hope, Birchover, Curbar and Hathersage, and the one at Hope was still in use as recently as 1967, when an astonishing total of about 300 stray sheep were impounded in a year. In 1947, 14 sheep strayed into four different gardens in Hope, where they tucked into vegetables and other produce. The sheep were impounded and released back to the farmer on payment of a fine.

A pinder or 'pinner' was responsible for the rounding up of stray livestock, impounding them in the pinfold and returning them to their owners for a fee. He could charge the owners of the stray animals for the feed he provided for them, as well as for any damage that had been caused to land belonging to others.

The charge for their recovery at the Hope pinfold in 1967 was two shillings and six pence (roughly £2.70 today) per head in the summer months (when grass was plentiful), and six pence a head in the winter, in addition to two pence (20p today) per head for the pinner. The owner risked a fine if he broke into the pinfold to retrieve his stock.

A 1940s notice on the well-preserved six-foot-high, gated pinfold at Hope by the Watersgate Bridge over Peakshole Water lists the regulations surrounding the use of the pinfold and the related costs. The impoundment system was governed by an ancient law relating to what was called 'distress damage feasant'.

Address Pinfold Road, Hope, Hope Valley, S33 6RD | **Getting there** Close to the Watersgate Bridge in the centre of Hope | **Hours** Accessible 24 hours | **Tip** A church was recorded at Hope in the Domesday Book of 1086, but the present St Peter's Church dates from the 14th and 15th centuries. It has two Anglo-Saxon preaching crosses in the churchyard, and inside, on the wall by the 14th-century font, are two 13th-century stone slabs showing horns, swords and arrows, which indicate they may have been on the graves of wood reeves, officials responsible for governing the medieval Royal Forest of the Peak.

65 Magpie Mine

The curse of Magpie Mine

When the wind whistles through the rusting winding gear and round the chimneys of Magpie Mine in the fields south of Sheldon, it can feel haunted by the ghosts of the lead miners who worked there, off and on, for 200 years.

It remains the best-preserved lead mine in the Peak, working at a time when the extraction of lead ore (galena) was one of the most important industries in the White Peak area, and local men worked a dual economy of farming in the summer months and mining in the winter.

But that sinister feeling that still hangs around the gaunt chimneys and skeletal ironwork is based on historical fact. The precious lead veins that underlie these now peaceful pastures were the scene of bitter disputes between rival groups of miners in the 19th century.

And in 1833, a dispute between the miners of the Great Redsoil and Maypitt veins led to the lighting of underground fires of tar and straw by the Maypitt men in an attempt to 'smoke out' their rivals. Three Redsoil miners died of asphyxiation in the choking, smoke-filled tunnels. According to one witness, smoke poured out of the shafts 'like Manchester factory chimneys'.

In the ensuing trial at Derby Assizes, all the Maypitt miners were acquitted, claiming the fires were only lit in self-defence after the Redsoil miners had lit them first. The result obviously fired a great deal of resentment in the area, and the widow of one of the dead miners cast a curse on the mine, which it is claimed still stands to this day.

The most prominent remains at Magpie today are the two chimneys from the former pumping engines – the square one built by local miners and the round one by Cornishmen – the circular powder house, the black-painted winding gear over the main shaft, the reconstructed horse gin and the mine manager's house, which is now run as a field study centre by the Peak District Mines Historical Society.

Address Magpie Mine, Sheldon, DE45 1QU | **Getting there** Signposted on the minor road off the B5065 Bakewell to Monyash road, three miles west of Bakewell | **Hours** Accessible 24 hours | **Tip** It's a pleasant, two-mile walk to Magpie across the fields from Sheldon, where the Cock & Pullet pub in the main street serves a hearty, traditional pub lunch (+44 (0) 1629 814292).

66 Mandale Mine

An Aztec ruin in a Jekyll and Hyde dale

Rising like an Aztec ruin from the ash woodlands of Lathkill Dale, the ivy-clad walls of Mandale Mine stand silent witness to the generations of lead miners who delved deep underground here to extract the precious lead ore.

Now a peaceful, beautiful National Nature Reserve, alive with birdsong and bright with wildflowers, it's hard to imagine that a century ago, the dale echoed to the sounds of industry, the shouting of miners and the rumble of horse-drawn wagons.

The Jekyll and Hyde nature of Lathkill Dale is one of its major attractions, making it the showpiece of Natural England's Derbyshire nature reserves and a favourite with the thousands of visitors who frequent the easy, two-mile trail which runs through it from Over Haddon to Monyash.

Mandale Mine is claimed to be one of the oldest and richest lead mines in the Peak and it was certainly working in the 13th century when the Inquisition into the Liberties and Customs of lead mining was laid down in 1288. In 1700, the workings were said to be 380 feet deep and two miles long.

The largest remaining mine building, reached just off the main path through the dale, is the now roofless bob wall of the Engine House. Behind it is a deep hollow that once housed a 35-foot-diameter water wheel, which was directly over the pumping shaft to the mine.

Further down the dale you will come across the remaining pillars of what was once an aqueduct that conveyed water from a channel on the southern side of the dale to power the water wheel at Mandale Mine. Also on the southern bank hidden amongst the trees are the restored remains of James Bateman's house. Bateman was the Lathkill Dale Mining Company's agent between 1836 and 1842.

The mine continued working off and on for an astonishing 500 years before finally closing in 1851, after making a loss of £36,000.

Address Near Over Haddon, DE45 1JE | **Getting there** A steep walk down the Dale Road from Over Haddon to reach the entrance to Lathkill Dale, next to a clapper bridge over the river; Mandale Mine is about half a mile away | **Hours** Viewable from the outside only (except for experienced cavers with advance permission) | **Tip** Mandale Mine miners would undoubtedly have enjoyed a pint at The Miners' Arms in School Lane, Over Haddon, which was owned by agent James Bateman. Now a family-run pub and restaurant known as The Lathkil Hotel (+44 (0) 1629 812501), it dates back to 1828 and enjoys splendid views across the dale towards the church tower of Youlgrave.

67 Middleton Top Engine House

Getting up steam at Middleton

It's still a long, hard pull for walkers and cyclists up the Sheep Pasture incline at the start of the High Peak Trail near Cromford. And it was an equally serious problem for Josiah Jessop when he set out to survey the Cromford and High Peak Railway in the early 19th century.

The Cromford and High Peak Railway was created by Act of Parliament in 1825 to link the Cromford Canal at Cromford with the Peak Forest Canal at Whaley Bridge. It was intended to provide a more direct through-route from the Midlands to Manchester, avoiding the tortuous Trent and Mersey Canal. In fact, and quite improbably, it was originally conceived as a canal and the railway's gradient profile was similar to that of a canal, with the stations described as 'wharfs'.

The first major hurdle that Jessop had to overcome was to engineer a way to get trains over Derbyshire's bleak White Peak plateau, which rises over 1,000 feet between the two canals. As is the case today, locomotives could not climb steeply inclined hills. Jessop's ingenious answer was a series of steam-powered inclined planes, hauling locos and their wagons up the incline.

The octagonal Middleton Top Engine House houses the oldest working beam engine of its type. The original pair of beam engines, built by the Butterley Company of Ripley in 1829, together with its massive boilers and imposing 100-foot chimney, remain and can be observed in operation during regular open days organised by Derbyshire County Council.

The Cromford and High Peak line was surveyed by Jessop in 1824, and the line was opened in 1831. It was 33 miles long, and one of the first long-distance railways to be built in Britain. It closed in 1967 and became the popular High Peak Trail walking, cycling and riding route.

Address Middleton Top Engine House and Countryside Centre, Rise End, Middleton, DE4 4LS, www.derbyshire.gov.uk/leisure/countryside/countryside.aspx | **Getting there** Easily reached from the High Peak Trail, signed off the minor road from Middleton to Wirksworth | **Hours** Check website for opening hours | **Tip** The Leawood Steam Pumphouse, over the A6 at the foot of the Sheep Pasture Incline, was built in 1849 to pump water from the River Derwent into Cromford Canal. It has regular steaming dates from Easter until October (+44 (0) 1629 533298).

68 Miller's Dale Lime Kilns

Brutalist buttresses

Looking for all the world like a Brutalist, Bauhaus-style block of flats, the massive buttresses of the Miller's Dale lime kilns tower menacingly above the popular Monsal Trail walking and riding route.

Constructed to make quicklime, they were ideally placed to use the locally available limestone as the raw material; the adjacent former Rowsley to Buxton Midland Railway line (now the Monsal Trail) both brought in the coal to fire the kilns and transported the quicklime away to the cities where it was needed.

Previously, quicklime had been produced in small kilns – many of which are still visible outside White Peak villages – and was mainly for agricultural use. But the huge increase in demand for quicklime, especially from the chemical and steel industries, meant the process demanded a more industrial solution.

The kilns on either side of the former Miller's Dale Station on the Monsal Trail were originally built in 1867 and became operational in 1880. The limestone was taken from quarries in the hills behind the kilns then transported the short distance to the kilns via hopper tubs on a narrow gauge track. They were then hauled up the incline and tipped into the kilns. The quicklime was then collected and taken by barrow to trucks on the Midland Line, which was constructed in the 1860s.

The massive concrete buttresses were added by the East Buxton Lime Company in the 1920s and quicklime production, which at its height amounted to about 50 tons a day from Miller's Dale, came to an end towards the end of the Second World War in 1944. The former Miller's Dale station was an important junction on the Midland Line, because it was the nearest railway station to the tourist and spa town of Buxton, to which it was linked by a branch line.

The station, which closed in 1968, is now a National Park car park.

Address Miller's Dale car park, Wormhill, Buxton, SK17 8SN | Getting there On the B6049 off the A6 between Bakewell and Buxton | Hours Viewable 24 hours | Tip The Anglers Rest, on the banks of the River Wye in Miller's Dale (+44 (0) 1298 871323), is a traditional 18th-century village pub in a delightful setting down a narrow lane on the banks of the River Wye.

69 Minninglow, High Peak Trail

High place for ancestors

If you know where to look, visible on the skyline in many views of the White Peak is the tree-crowned 1,213-foot hilltop of Minninglow, just off the High Peak Trail between Parwich and Elton. Within the surrounding circular clump of trees and watched over by some ancient and decaying beeches are the remains of a huge Neolithic chambered tomb and two Bronze Age bowl barrows.

The chambered tomb is the highest and largest in the Peak and started life as a small mound with a single chamber. It was then covered by an oval cairn measuring 148 feet by 125 feet, surviving to a height of over seven feet. It now contains two complete burial chambers made of limestone slabs complete with their capstones, and at least three other incomplete chambers. Pevsner described the site in his *Buildings of England: Derbyshire* (1953) as 'dominating the landscape in its location and magnificent scale'. The site was chosen by our Neolithic forefathers for good reason. It commands a prominent point of reference and focus to the south on the edge of the White Peak limestone plateau and over the valley towards Wirksworth.

The tomb was excavated by Thomas Bateman in 1843 and 1851 and has been described as one of the most impressive of Derbyshire's surviving prehistoric burials. The oldest chamber dates from the Early Neolithic period, but other finds indicate its use in the Late Neolithic or early Bronze Age, and even into the Roman period. The two bowl barrows, also excavated by Bateman, date from the Bronze Age and also show signs of Roman disturbance.

As our Neolithic ancestors had realised, before the surrounding band of trees grew up, the view from Minninglow was exceptional, extending as far south as the Shropshire and Malvern Hills.

Address Minninglow car park, DE4 2PR | **Getting there** Via the A5012 Newhaven to Cromford road. A 200-yard signposted concessionary path leads from the High Peak Trail and there are wooden markers on the route to the tomb | **Hours** Viewable 24 hours | **Tip** About half a mile northwest of Minninglow is the massive Minninglow Embankment on the High Peak Trail. This Grade II-listed structure was constructed from local limestone in the 1820s. There is access from the car park and picnic site about 200 yards further along the High Peak Trail.

70 Monsal Dale Viaduct

The 'foolish' viaduct

The prospect of the Monsal Dale, or Headstone, viaduct from Monsal Head is regularly voted one of the finest and most popular views in the Peak District. The 300-foot-long, five-arched viaduct was built in the early 1860s to carry the Midland Line between London and Manchester and famously attracted the wrath of the pioneering conservationist and critic John Ruskin.

Writing in his *Fors Clavigera* bulletin to the workers of Britain in the 1870s, Ruskin fumed that the viaduct had been constructed through a valley which was once the haunt of the Gods so that 'every fool in Buxton can be in Bakewell in half an hour, and every fool in Bakewell at Buxton'.

But that soaring viaduct beneath the prominent north-facing escarpment of hillfort-topped Fin Cop is now very much an integral part of the scene. It was once touched out of a photograph of Monsal Head by a National Park photographer, and few people could recognise the scene or the location without the viaduct which had so offended the purist senses of John Ruskin.

The construction of the Midland Line between Rowsley and Buxton was one of the greatest challenges facing the Midland Railway in its attempt to provide a new London to Manchester route in the 1860s. The valley of the River Wye was chosen as the best alternative, although because of the steep-sided Monsal and Chee Dales, it required an expensive series of tunnels and viaducts, the most famous of which was that at Monsal Head.

The Midland Line eventually closed in 1968 and was bought by the National Park Authority in 1980 and converted to the popular Monsal Trail for walkers, cyclists and horse riders. In recent years, the series of tunnels on the route have been illuminated, making it an exciting experience for cyclists and walkers, young and old. Ambitious plans to re-open the line have so far proved unsuccessful.

Address Little Longstone, Bakewell, DE45 1NL | Getting there The Monsal Dale viaduct is on the Monsal Trail, a walking and riding route converted from the former Midland Line and an easy three-mile walk from Bakewell; alternatively, limited parking at Monsal Head, off the B6465 Ashford to Wardlow road, and then a steep descent through woodland to reach the viaduct | Hours Accessible 24 hours | Tip The bold escarpment facing you when looking across Monsal Head is Fin Cop, which is crowned by a promontory hillfort where archaeologists recently discovered the scene of an Iron Age massacre.

71 Navio Roman Fort

Outpost of empire

The major interest of the Romans during their 300-year occupation of the Peak District was its plentiful reserves of lead, used throughout the empire for roofing and plumbing. And the administrative and defensive centre for the Roman lead industry in the Peak was the fort of Navio, on a prominent bend in the River Noe at Brough-on-Noe in the Hope Valley.

Recent archaeological excavations have revealed the fort had a massive associated civil settlement, or *vicus,* just outside its walls, where a sizeable civilian population served the needs of the legionnaires posted to the fort, some of whom are known from an inscribed dedication to have come from Aquitaine, now in south-western France. Other finds included the foundations of several large, stone-built buildings, two stone ballista balls and Roman coins and pottery.

The only major archaeological investigation of the fort itself was carried out in the 1930s by Sir Ian Richmond and J. P. Gillam. It established that there had been at least three successive forts on the same site. The original, built of timber and earthworks in around A.D. 80 was rebuilt in stone in a rectangular form (about 295 feet by 344 feet) in around A.D. 150, and occupied for over 200 years. The fort was subsequently rebuilt and altered and still in use until around A.D. 350.

An earlier excavation in 1903 uncovered steps to an underground stone-walled chamber, probably used as a strongroom to store valuables or money, below the *Principia* or headquarters building. A large Centurial stone and a gritstone altar were also found in the fort's strongroom. The stone was erected 'in honour of the Emperor Caesar Titus Aelius Hadrianus Antoninus Augustus Pius', and the altar is dedicated to the goddess Arnemetia, who is remembered in the sacred mineral spring waters of *Aquae Arnemetiae*, modern-day Buxton.

Address Brough-on-Noe, Hope Valley, S33 9HG | Getting there Signposted by an ancient Peak & Northern footpath sign (No. 38, dated 1908) off the B6049 Bradwell to Brough road | Hours Accessible 24 hours | Tip Ye Olde Bowling Green Inn in Smalldale, Bradwell (+44 (0) 1433 627539) dates from 1577. This traditional half-timbered pub is dog friendly and oozes charm, with stunning views and open fires in the winter.

72 Odin Mine

Stemples of doom

Odin Mine, an ominous, evil-looking, tree-topped cleft in the rocks near the old road beneath Mam Tor, claims to be one of the oldest recorded lead mines in the country, first recorded in 1280. But its name, echoing that of the Norse god of death, wisdom, magic and madness, seems to suggest it might have been worked for at least 1,000 years, possibly even by the Romans. The Romans certainly had great need for lead for their plumbing systems, and they mined the galena extensively during their occupation of Britain. So it's not beyond the bounds of possibility that Odin Mine was originally worked by them.

In the early 18th century Richard Bagshawe had a considerable stake in Odin Mine and his family retained their interest in it until the 1850s. The mine was worked continuously throughout the 18th century with annual ore extraction varying between 100 and 800 tonnes per annum.

The place certainly has an evil reputation among cavers, described in an official guide as 'unstable and potentially dangerous'. Added to that, it is claimed to be haunted by the ghost of one of the murderers of Allan and Clara in the Winnats Pass, and by the spirits of 70 local miners, who drowned there after an underground flood.

The furthest reaches of the mine are reached via a 35-foot drop and ducking under rotten wooden 'stemples' (beams holding up waste material) to eventually reach the Cartgate Chamber, with its beautiful stone-arched roof, a miracle of underground construction. It was made by miners with no lighting but a candle stuffed into their hats.

Odin Mine is, of course, fenced off and out of reach of the casual tourist, but just a glance into its Stygian depths should be enough to put any sane person off even thinking about entering. Nearby are the remains of a 19th-century circular horse gin and crushing wheel, used to crush the lead ore (galena) extracted from the mine.

Address Odin Mine, Castleton, Hope Valley, S33 8WA | Getting there From the bus turning area at the end of the closed Mam Tor road, go west through the gate towards the large worked-out rake; the obvious large entrance to Odin Mine is on the left | Hours Accessible 24 hours | Tip The now-closed Mam Tor road above Odin Mine shows an impressive and ever-widening landslip which closed this as the main road to Chapel-en-le-Frith in the 1970s.

73 Ore House

Where the ore was stored

Standing like an abandoned garage out in the White Peak countryside between Winster and Pikehall is the best-preserved lead ore house in the Peak District. It was used by local lead mine owners for keeping their lead ore (galena) safe while awaiting measurement by the official Barmaster from the Barmote Court. His job was to assess the amount of duty – or 'lot' – payable to the local lord of the lead field.

Ore houses would have been built at or near the mines, and the landscape around the Winster ore house is riddled with the remains of many former lead mines. There is a record of Benjamin Wyatt building an ore house at Watergrove Mine, near Follow, as early as the 1780s, and the Winster one dates from around 1800.

Every six weeks or so, after a sufficient quantity of ore had been raised, the Barmaster would go to the mine to measure the ore and take a proportion of duty ore. Traditionally, this was every thirteenth dish, although the proportion varied in the different lead fields.

According to lead mining historian Lynn Willies: '[Winster Ore House] would have been convenient for the mid to late 18th-century Barmasters (the Roberts, father and son), who, I think, lived just down the road in the cottages below the Miners Standard.'

The mine owners stored their lead ore by using the chute at the back of the ore house, and the roof is barrel-vaulted for additional security. Large doors at the front have been replaced by a grill so that the chute and interior are visible.

An interpretive panel was added to the grilled entrance to the Winster Ore House by the Peak District National Park authority in the 1980s, and describes its former use and history. Water is a precious commodity on the fast-draining limestone plateau, and across the road from the Ore House is Mosey Mere, which provided water for the former small hamlet of Islington Green, where some of the lead miners lived.

Address The Ore House, Bank Top, Winster, DE4 2DR | Getting there The Ore House is beside the B5056 about half a mile from The Miners Standard pub | Hours Accessible 24 hours | Tip Lead miners undoubtedly quenched their thirst at The Miners Standard, Bank Top, Winster (+44 (0) 1629 650279), originally built as a farmhouse around 1653.

74 Peak Cavern

The village that never saw the sun

Until the young Queen Victoria's visit in 1842, Peak Cavern, said to be the largest cave entrance in Britain, was anciently known as 'The Devil's Arse' (a name to which it recently reverted) and the river which emerges from it (Peakshole Water) as the River Styx. The name may have arisen because of the occasional flatulent-sounding noises coming from inside the cave in times of flood, but it was changed so as not to cause offence to the prim and proper young Queen.

The huge gaping maw beneath the beetling cliffs on which stand the ruins of Peveril Castle was one of the original Wonders of the Peak, extolled by Thomas Hobbes and Charles Cotton. The entrance arch is 115 feet wide and 50 feet high, and what is known as the 'vestibule' stretches back more than 300 feet. This enormous entrance passage was used for at least 400 years by a community of ropemakers, some of whom lived 'in a village that never saw the sun' in huts against the west wall. It has been used in recent years to host Christmas carol concerts and pop concerts, and even as a cinema.

The cave was also known as a refuge for bandits, and it was the scene of a legendary meeting between Cock Lorel, leader of the outlaws, and Giles Hather, King of the Gypsies, where they invented a thieves' cant (or language).

Visitors can take a guided exploration of some of the initial chambers of the cave, including the aptly named Lumbago Walk (you have to bend low to pass through), the Great Cave and Roger Rain's House.

Caves explored by experienced cavers extend 10 miles beyond the visitors' route to make the Peak Cavern system one of the longest in Britain. Another record was added to Peak Cavern's portfolio in 1999 when Titan Shaft was discovered – at 464 feet, it is the deepest natural shaft yet found in Britain.

Address Peak Cavern, Castleton, Hope Valley, S33 8WP, +44 (0) 1433 620285, www.peakspeedwell.info/index.php/access-information/peak-cavern-access | **Getting there** Access is by a signed cul-de-sac leading off Goosehill in the centre of Castleton | **Hours** Public access to Peak Cavern is available year round, but must be pre-booked via the website | **Tip** Castleton has three other popular show caves: Treak Cliff (+44 (0) 1433 620571), Speedwell (+44 (0) 1433 623018) and Blue John (+44 (0) 1433 620638).

75 Penelope Boothby Tomb

Bringing a queen to tears

The moving inscription on the tomb of five-year-old Penelope Boothby in the Boothby Chapel of St Oswald's Church, Ashbourne, reads: *She was in form and intellect most exquisite. The unfortunate Parents ventured their all on this frail Bark and the wreck was total.* The lifelike white Carrara marble effigy of the young girl, seemingly peacefully asleep, is considered the masterpiece of the renowned 18th-century sculptor Thomas Banks, and supposedly brought Queen Charlotte to tears when she saw it at a Royal Academy exhibition.

Penelope, who died in 1791, was the daughter of Sir Brooke Boothby, 6th Baronet, who lived at the now demolished Ashbourne Hall. Sir Brooke was a minor poet and published several sonnets on his daughter's death, and it was said that he never recovered from the tragic loss. The Boothby monument forms the centrepiece to the Boothby Chapel, which also contains many other older monuments to the locally prominent Boothby, Cokayne and Bradbourne families, some in armour and dating back to the 14th century.

The graceful 212-foot spire of St Oswald's dominates the town, and the church was referred to by George Eliot in *Adam Bede* (1859) as the 'finest mere parish church in England'. James Boswell, a regular visitor to the town with his friend Dr Samuel Johnson, said the church was 'one of the largest and most luminous that I have seen in any town of the same size'.

A rare brass plaque in the south transept commemorates its dedication on 24 April, 1241 by Hugh de Pateshull, Bishop of Coventry and Lichfield. Probably replacing earlier Saxon and Norman churches, construction of the present church in the Early English, Perpendicular and Decorated styles continued until the early 14th century.

The other great glory of St Oswald's is its stained glass, including beautiful Arts and Crafts windows by Christopher Whall, Charles Eamer Kempe and John Hardman.

Address St Oswald's Parish Church, Mayfield Road, Ashbourne, DE6 1AR | **Getting there** At the end of Ashbourne's main street | **Hours** Church open daily 10am–5pm | **Tip** It's probably best to avoid Ashbourne on Shrove Tuesday and Ash Wednesday, when shops are boarded up and the streets are taken over by the rough-and-tumble Royal Shrovetide Football Match, which is said to be a forerunner of today's football. Played between teams representing the 'Up'ards' and the 'Down'ards', the dividing line being the Henmore Brook, the 'goals' are three miles apart.

76 Peter's Stone

The last gibbeting in England

Peter's Stone is a detached, dome-like block of limestone that has slipped away from the side of Cressbrook Dale, just off the A623 Chesterfield to Chapel-en-le-Frith road at Wardlow Mires. It is supposed to have taken its name from its similarity to St Peter's Basilica in far-off Rome.

But it has a more sinister reputation as the site of reputedly the last public gibbeting in England in 1815. The unfortunate victim was 21-year-old Anthony Lingard, who had been convicted of the murder of Hannah Oliver, the tollkeeper at nearby Wardlow Mires.

Lingard was convicted on the key evidence of Hannah's missing red shoes. Local cobbler, a Mr Marsden of Stoney Middleton, confirmed that a pair of shoes found at Lingard's house had been made for Hannah.

Following his conviction at Derby Assizes and execution by hanging, Lingard's body was hung in chains in an iron cage from April Fool's Day 1815 and remained there for 11 years – a grisly reminder to passersby of the force of the law. Apparently, hundreds of people flocked to see the morbid spectacle, and pedlars and hucksters even erected booths to sell souvenirs.

One such passerby was William Newton, the famed 'Minstrel of the Peak' who, when he accidentally came across the gruesome sight, was so appalled by its inhumanity that he wrote a poem about it, in which Lingard's father paid an imagined nocturnal visit to the site. Apparently, this provided a huge boost to his campaign for penal reform, which eventually led to the ultimate abolition of the barbarous punishment of gibbeting in 1834.

Lingard's skeleton was finally removed in 1826, apparently following complaints from local people about the gruesome clattering of his bones in the wind. And on a windy night, it is said they can still be heard.

Address The nearest postcode for Peter's Stone is SK17 8RW | Getting there About three miles west of Stoney Middleton on the A623 Chesterfield to Chapel-en-le-Frith road; a short walk up the dale to reach Peter's Stone | Hours Accessible 24 hours | Tip The Three Stags' Head at Wardlow Mires is a characterful and unspoilt 300-year-old pub with stone-flagged floors and low ceilings (+44 (0) 1298 872268).

77 Peveril Castle

William's lofty stronghold

The four-square keep of Peveril Castle has dominated views of its eponymous village of Castleton at the head of the Hope Valley for 850 years. First mentioned in the *Domesday Book*, Peveril Castle is one of England's most spectacularly sited and earliest stone-built Norman fortresses, originally built by William Peveril, an illegitimate son of William the Conqueror.

William was Steward of the medieval Royal Forest of the Peak, a 180-square-mile hunting reserve, the exclusive preserve of the King and his acolytes. As Steward, William was charged with enacting the brutal forest laws, which included castration, blinding or the cutting off of a limb for anyone caught hunting in the king's preserve. He also collected the revenues from the local lead mines.

The original castle was built shortly after the Norman Conquest in the date every schoolchild remembers (1066) and was unusual in that it had stone walls from the outset. Most early castles, of the motte-and-bailey type, were built of wood. It was much strengthened and the keep added by Henry II in 1176. Henry visited Peveril Castle many times, apparently holding tournaments and once hosting King Malcolm IV of Scotland there. A curtain wall surrounds the keep, which teeters on the precipitous edge of Cave Dale and the gaping maw of Peak Cavern. It was granted to John of Gaunt in 1372 and was described as 'ruinous' by the 16th century. Recent archaeological investigations have revealed a substantial settlement consisting of a hall, barns and stables in the enclosed inner bailey. The kids will doubtless enjoy the medieval garderobe (toilet) in the keep being pointed out.

The steep climb to the castle at the top of the hill overlooking the village is rewarded with breathtaking views over the head of the Hope Valley towards the Great Ridge of Mam Tor with its encircling hillfort, Back Tor and Lose Hill, and also the tor-topped Win Hill.

Address Market Place, Castleton, S33 8WQ, www.english-heritage.org.uk/visit/places/peveril-castle | Getting there On the A625 a mile west of Hope | Hours Check website for seasonal opening hours | Tip Castleton is the home of the unique semi-precious mineral Blue John, and you can visit any of the four spectacular show caves and their shops in and around the village. They are: Peak Cavern (+44 (0) 1433 620285), Treak Cliff (+44 (0) 1433 620571), Blue John (+44 (0) 1433 620638) and Speedwell (+44 (0) 1433 623018).

78 Pilsbury Castle

A Norman's home

Pilsbury Castle, in the remote valley of the Upper Dove, is the best example of a Norman motte and bailey castle in the Peak District.

Situated beside a prominent, tree-topped reef limestone knoll, it is unusual in having three outer baileys (fortified outer enclosures) rather than the usual one. Originally built in earthworks and timber as the administrative centre of the de Ferriers family in the late 11th or early 12th century, it effectively commanded the Upper Dove and a strategic crossing point of the river.

By the 13th century however, the township of Hartington, two miles downstream, had been established as the main market centre by William de Ferriers, Earl of Derby. In fact, Hartington has the earliest recorded market charter in the Peak, granted by King John to de Ferriers in 1203, giving him the right to hold a Wednesday market and a three-day fair on the festival of the parish church's patron saint, St Giles. But Pilsbury was still in use for manorial courts well into the 19th century.

Quite why the de Ferriers should have chosen such an isolated place to build the first castle has been debated for years. Following the Norman conquest, the area around Pilsbury was granted to Henry de Ferrers by King William. The Upper Dove area was devastated during William's infamous Harrying of the North, and the castle may have been built by Henry in the aftermath, to establish control of the area. Alternatively, it may have been built by Robert de Ferriers or his father during the 12th-century period known as 'The Anarchy' for, while the de Ferriers supported Stephen, the neighbouring Earl of Chester supported the Empress Matilda.

Either way, Pilsbury Castle remains a highly evocative place, accessible via a walled lane from the hamlet of Pilsbury, two miles north of Hartington. A National Park interpretive board explains the history of the castle.

Address Pilsbury Castle, Hartington, SK17 0AB | Getting there Signposted on the lane from Pilsbury hamlet, two miles north of Hartington | Hours Accessible 24 hours | Tip There's no pub in Pilsbury, but the Charles Cotton Hotel in Hartington's Market Place (+44 (0) 7835 126076) is a characterful, early 17th-century hostelry named after Izaak Walton's fishing companion, on the nearby River Dove.

79 Postbox, Little Longstone

Wait a minute, Mr Postman

The rather battered and severely over-painted scarlet wall-mounted letter box in Little Longstone is a real rarity. Barely discernible at the top is the royal cypher of King Edward VIII ('E VIII R'), one of the shortest-reigning British monarchs ever – his controversial reign lasted only 326 days.

There were 271 letter boxes made during the reign of Edward VIII. Of these, apparently only six were wall boxes like this one, 161 were pillar boxes, and the remaining 104 were those used in sub-post offices. After his abdication in 1936 – in order to marry American divorcée Wallis Simpson – most boxes bearing his cypher were either modified or replaced.

Edward, the eldest child of the Duke and Duchess of York, later King George V and Queen Mary, was born in 1894 during the reign of his great-grandmother Queen Victoria. He was made Prince of Wales on his 16th birthday and the Prince gained widespread popular support due to his charm and charisma – even his fashion sense became a hallmark of the era. On his father's death in 1936, Edward became the second monarch of the House of Windsor. But months into his reign, he caused a constitutional crisis by his proposal to marry Wallis Simpson, an American who had divorced her first husband and was seeking a divorce from her second. At the time, a monarch was not allowed to marry someone who had been divorced.

When it became apparent he could not marry Wallis and remain on the throne, Edward abdicated, movingly stating that he found it impossible to carry the burden of responsibility and discharge his duties as king 'without the help and support of the woman I love'. He was succeeded by his younger brother, who became George VI. He married Wallis in 1937, and after the war they spent the rest of their lives in France. They remained married until his death in 1972.

Address Little Longstone, SK17 8SN | Getting there The village is on a minor road west of Great Longstone, just off the B6465 from Ashford-in-the-Water to Wardlow | Hours Viewable 24 hours | Tip The 16th-century Packhorse Inn at Little Longstone (+44 (0) 1629 640471), was recently voted by Tripadvisor as one of the Top 10 Cosiest Pubs in Britain. Traditional local ales and no less than three open fires make this a really welcoming pub for walkers using the Monsal Trail.

80 Riley Graves

Tragic story of the loss of a family

Eyam (pronounced 'Eem' as in stream) cannot escape from its tragic past because it will always be saddled with the epithet of The Plague Village. The heroic, self-imposed quarantine by the villagers after the Bubonic Plague struck during the years 1665–66 has been called 'the greatest epic in the annals of rural life', and the village is today always associated with the tragic so-called 'visitation'.

During a 14-month period between September 1665 and November 1666, a total of 259 Eyam villagers died of the Plague and in some cases, whole families were wiped out. It is thought that the virus arrived in Eyam in a box of cloth brought from London by George Viccars, a journeyman tailor.

Many cottages in the village are still marked with plaques recording the names of the victims, and a record of their names is also kept in the parish church of St Lawrence, ensuring that the epic story of the self-imposed sacrifice that the villagers made will never be forgotten.

Led by their minister, William Mompesson, and his non-conformist predecessor, the Rev Thomas Stanley, the villagers self-imposed a quarantine and ban on movement so that the deadly virus would not spread through the rest of the county. Some of the pitiful graves of the victims can be seen in the fields around the village, because residents were not allowed to be buried in the churchyard during the 'visitation'.

One such Eyam family that was particularly tragically hit by the Plague were the Hancocks of Riley House Farm, six of whom died within a week of each other in August 1665. The distraught mother had to bury her husband, two sons and three daughters in the fields close to the farm. The evocative headstones marking their graves can still be seen grouped inside a walled enclosure known as the Riley Graves, just a short walk outside the village.

Address Riley Lane, Eyam, S32 5AE | Getting there Riley Lane is off the minor road leading east towards Grindleford; limited parking on site, but more in the village | Hours Accessible 24 hours | Tip Eyam Museum (www.eyam-museum.org.uk) in the former Methodist Chapel in Hawkhill Road, has exhibits and displays which graphically tell the story of the village from prehistoric to modern times, plus the harrowing story of the Eyam Plague.

81 Round Building

Cutting it fine at Hathersage

The site of the former village gasworks just outside the Hope Valley village of Hathersage was becoming a bit of an eyesore. Erected between 1906–7, the gas holder had faithfully served the village until mains gas arrived, but now the circular, five-acre site lay derelict.

But for the award-winning Sheffield cutlery and streetwear designer David Mellor, it represented an opportunity to realise a long-held ambition of building a new, purpose-built cutlery factory. The circular footprint was perfectly suited to the manufacture of cutlery, allowing for an anticlockwise progression round the factory, moving from the cutting and grinding of metals to hand-finishing processes and the final stages of cleaning and packing.

Mellor commissioned his friend, the award-winning architect Sir Michael Hopkins, to design his new factory, which was described as 'a minor masterpiece of modern architecture' and received numerous prestigious architectural and environmental awards.

Hopkins' aim was to combine traditional materials with modern structural techniques, resulting in a building that is highly functional and technologically advanced but which also enhances its setting. Built of stone with a conical lead roof, the building has a circular clerestory window and central lantern, which allows natural light to enter the interior.

Hopkins was also chosen as the designer of the converted 19th-century Retort House and glass-fronted Design Museum, shop and restaurant, which opened in 2006. The internal fixtures were designed by Mellor's son, Corin, who is now Creative Director of the company.

Children (and many adults) will love the working set of David Mellor-designed traffic lights in the restaurant, and also the bus stop, seats and other street furniture, which he also designed, outside. A permanent exhibition of Mellor's silver and stainless steel work is also featured in the restaurant.

Address The Round Building, Hathersage, Sheffield, S32 1BA, +44 (0) 1433 650220 | Getting there About half a mile outside Hathersage on the B6001 Grindleford road | Hours Mon–Sat 10am–5pm, Sun 11am–5pm | Tip 'Outside' is the appropriate name of the Peak's best outdoor equipment shop in Hathersage's Main Road (+44 (0) 1433 651936). It carries a comprehensive range of clothing, boots and gear.

82 Saxon Cross, Eyam

A truncated treasure

The Peak District is blessed with a fine group of Saxon, or Celtic, wayside crosses – claimed to be as fine a collection as anywhere outside Northumberland. Scholars believe that in the 8th and 9th centuries there must have been a school of dedicated craftsmen producing the early Christian wayside preaching markers found at places such as Bakewell, Hope, Edale and on the eastern moors.

One of the finest and most reproduced is the eight-foot-high Saxon Cross that stands in St Lawrence's churchyard in the plague village of Eyam. But many visitors don't realise that what they see today is a truncated version of the original, with the lower arm of the angel-capped crosshead missing. The truncated version was innocently copied by the village of nearby Grindleford when it constructed its war memorial in 1921.

Dating from the 8th to the 9th century, Eyam Cross was possibly originally set up at Cross Low on the moors northwest of the village. Like most, it was originally a wayside preaching cross, which must have once stood 10 feet high. The cross was rediscovered beside a trackway on the moors in the 18th century, and taken into the churchyard, where for a long time it stood abandoned. Eventually however, its importance was recognised, and it was restored and placed in the churchyard, where it now proudly stands beside two clipped yew trees.

It is said to be the only one of its type in the Midlands that at least partially retains its cross-head. It has rich decorations on its west face with typically Mercian interlacing scrollwork running up the shaft. Also in the upper section of the west face, there are carved figures – probably the Virgin with the baby Jesus, angels and Christ in glory, each in their own sections.

In addition to its many reminders of the 1665 visitation of the Plague, the 13th-century church of St Lawrence also houses a circular Norman font.

Address St Lawrence Church, Church Street, Eyam, S32 5QH | Getting there Eyam is signposted off the A623 Chesterfield to Chapel-en-le-Frith road as it leaves Stoney Middleton | Hours Accessible 24 hours | Tip Close to the Eyam's Saxon Cross in the churchyard is the table-top tomb of vicar's wife Catherine Mompesson, who died in the year of the Plague.

83 Sheepwash Bridge

Popular for Poohsticks

One of the most photographed places in the Peak District, the 18th-century, three-arched former packhorse Sheepwash Bridge at Ashford-in-the-Water, just north of Bakewell, is surely on every visitor's must-see list.

The three shallow limestone arches span the River Wye between two parapets, and the wall on the opposite side to the village swings round in a graceful arch to enclose the sheep pen, which gives a clue to how the bridge got its name.

Lambs were put into the pen and their mothers unceremoniously tossed into the river by shepherds on the village side and encouraged to swim across the fast-flowing water to get to them, thus cleaning their fleeces before their annual shearing.

Sleek rainbow and brown trout glide through the crystal-clear waters of the Wye around the bridge, which was recently named by Visit England as the best place in the country to play the popular family game of Poohsticks. A. A. Milne's 'bear of little brain' Winnie the Pooh's favourite game was floating sticks under a bridge on a flowing stream to see whose stick emerged on the other side first.

With its lovely, chocolate-box, window-boxed limestone cottages, Ashford itself is certainly worth a visit. The originally 13th-century parish church of Holy Trinity sports a rare Norman tympanum and contains several examples of Ashford Black Marble, a polished, fossil-filled limestone that became very popular during the reign of Queen Victoria, especially after the death of her husband Prince Albert. Ashford was once the centre of production for this mineral, extracted from quarries and mines in the vicinity.

In June every year, villagers of Ashford get together to create four different well dressings, the mosaic works of folk art entirely made from natural materials, which stand for about a week and attract thousands of visitors.

Address Sheepwash Bridge, Fennel Street, Ashford-in-the-Water, DE45 1QG | Getting there About a mile west of Bakewell, on the A6 | Hours Accessible 24 hours | Tip Claimed to be the 'quirkiest stately home in the UK', Thornbridge Hall (+44 (0) 1629 640617) is a Grade II-listed 18th-century mansion set in 80 acres of beautiful parkland. It has 10 acres of formal gardens, a café and a variety of playgrounds to amuse the kids.

84 Solly's Seat

Memories of a mill manager

An ornate stone seat has provided welcome relief for walkers and cyclists struggling up the steep Bottom Hill Road out of Cressbrook Dale in the Wye Valley for over a century. Solly's Seat – as it is known – is a moving memorial to Charles Solly, a former manager of Cressbrook Mill who tragically died at the tender age of 33 in 1898. The inscription reads: 'In memory of Charles Edward Solly. For 8 years in charge of The Cressbrook Mill. Died 5th January, 1898 aged 33. The memory of the Just is Blessed'.

The seat was funded by Mary Worthington, a much-loved and respected benefactor to the village, and daughter of Henry McConnel, who owned the cotton mill from 1835. Previously, 167 mostly orphaned girls had served as apprentices there, but McConnel brought in a skilled and professional workforce, and was a rarity among millowners, being renowned for the enlightened attitude he had for the care and welfare of his workers.

Before McConnel's ownership, the village was just a collection of buildings in the immediate vicinity of the mill. But when McConnel's workforce objected to the quality of their housing, he took it upon himself to build the Swiss-style model village that became the charming village that is Cressbrook today. The cottages cluster together on the steep wooded hillside, which many years ago was harvested for its crop of lilies of the valley, which were transported by train and sold in the Manchester markets.

Cressbrook Mill itself, originally founded by Richard Arkwright but later developed into its splendid, 12-bay Georgian country house style by William Newton, is now converted into luxury apartments. The building of Cressbrook village started in the late 1830s and was extended in 1902 by Mary to include a village club, which was modelled on a working men's club, and is still active today. Solly's Seat was restored by the Peak District National Park Authority in 1989.

Address Cressbrook, SK17 8SX | Getting there Take the minor road off the B6465 at Monsal Head | Hours Accessible 24 hours | Tip Cressbrook Mill, just downstream from the village, is a 12-bayed, classically pedimented and cupola-topped structure, built in 1815 and now converted into luxury apartments.

85 Solomon's Temple

A tower with a view

Prominent in so many views from Buxton, England's highest market town, Solomon's Temple is a castellated Victorian folly perched on the 1,440-foot summit of Grin Low, just to the south of the town.

Reached in a short, 20-minute climb from Poole's Cavern through the Grin Low Woods local nature reserve, the 20-foot-high, two-storey tower commands spectacular 360-degree views across the spa town and the surrounding countryside. In good conditions, you can see for 15 miles, beyond the impressive dome of the former Devonshire Hospital. On the northern horizon you can see Mam Tor at Castleton, and beyond that, Kinder Scout, at 2,088 feet the highest point in Derbyshire and the Peak District.

The original tower was built by Solomon Mycock, a local farmer and owner of the Cheshire Cheese Hotel (now Ye Olde Cheshire Cheese Inn) in the town's High Street, in the early 19th century, as an eyecatcher for visitors. But Solomon's original 'temple' fell into a ruinous state, and in 1894 a meeting of the local council at Buxton Town Hall decided they should try to rebuild the iconic local landmark. Discussions with the landowner, William Cavendish, the 7th Duke of Devonshire, decided that the reconstruction would be possible if the townspeople of Buxton chipped in to make up sufficient funding. Sketches of the proposed tower were submitted by architects W. R. Bryden and G. E. Garlick, and the plans were confirmed by the Duke. He subscribed £25 towards rebuilding the folly, adding to the £50 that Buxton had already donated.

The laying of the foundation stone in May 1896 was by all accounts a grand occasion. Witnessed by a large crowd, the stone was laid with due ceremony by local MP Colonel Sidebottom. The tower was eventually opened by the Duke's nephew, Victor Cavendish (later the 9th Duke of Devonshire), in September that year. The by now Grade II-listed tower was again restored in 1988.

Address Off Green Lane, Buxton, SK17 9DH | Getting there A brisk 20-minute walk from the Poole's Cavern car park | Hours Accessible 24 hours | Tip One of the original Wonders of the Peak, Poole's Cavern (+44 (0) 1298 26978) is one of the most interesting and spectacular show caves in the Peak District. Don't miss the Cathedral Chamber, Poached Egg formations, and Mary, Queen of Scots' chamber (she was allegedly an early visitor).

86__St Ann's Well

Waters of the goddess

It's a common sight to see people queuing up with containers and bottles alongside the shrine to St Ann at the foot of The Slopes at Buxton, filling them with the warm, mineral-rich and slightly effervescent water from the lion's head spout. A statue of St Ann with her young daughter Mary, mother of Jesus, watches over the scene with a look of benevolent benediction.

People have been 'taking the waters' at Buxton for at least 2,000 years, starting with the spa-loving Romans, who named the town *Aquae Arnemetiae* ('waters of the goddess of the grove'), probably borrowing the name from a Celtic water goddess. The Romans built a bath at the thermal spring site which is now under the west wing of John Carr's elegant, recently renovated Crescent. The Crescent, now a boutique hotel, was built for the 5th Duke of Devonshire between 1779 and 1789, and an excavation of the main spring in the 1970s uncovered a votive offering of Roman coins.

Some of the earliest illustrations of Buxton show a chapel and shrine to St Ann on the site of the present well, and during the 16th century the well and warm baths became a place of pilgrimage for infirm pilgrims hoping for a miracle cure. All this 'idolatry and superstition' was put to a stop by Henry VIII's reforming commissioners. Then George Talbot, 6th Earl of Shrewsbury, built the New Hall (paradoxically now known as the Old Hall) possibly to house his noble prisoner, Mary Queen of Scots.

Boosted by his profits from Ecton Hill copper mine in Staffordshire, Talbot's successor, the 5th Duke of Devonshire, embarked on an ambitious programme to re-build Buxton, to make it a spa to rival Bath. In addition to the Crescent, he built the Great Stables and Riding School (now part of the University of Derby) – which, at the time, had the largest unsupported dome in the world – and the elegant Georgian parish church of St John the Baptist.

Address The Crescent, Buxton, SK17 6BQ | Getting there St Ann's Well is situated at the bottom of The Slopes and opposite The Crescent in Buxton | Hours Accessible 24 hours | Tip Bring a bottle to sample Buxton's famed spring water from St Ann's Well – and it's free!

87 St John the Baptist, Matlock Dale

Vision of medieval sanctity

This often-overlooked gem is tucked away in a side lane off the busy A6 road between Matlock Bath and Matlock. With its charming mullioned-lighted oriel window and lead-covered, pyramidal-roofed bell turret overlooking the lane, it stands like a vision of medieval sanctity. It was, however, constructed as late as 1897 – at the height of the Arts and Crafts movement – as a private chapel for Mrs Louisa Sophia Harris. The designer was the prominent Arts and Crafts architect Guy Dawber, who lived locally at the time, and strangely, it was the only church he ever designed.

Dawber is probably best known for designing the Reptile House at London Zoo in Regent's Park, which opened in 1927. President of the Royal Institute of British Architects from 1925 to 1927, he was awarded the RIBA Royal Gold Medal in 1928. In 1926 he had played a prominent role in establishing the Council (now the Campaign) for the Preservation of Rural England (CPRE) and became its first president.

The chapel, standing on a vertical limestone retaining wall that towers above the lane, is recorded in the National Heritage List as a designated Grade II*-listed building. Since 2002 it has been under the care of the Friends of Friendless Churches and the charity has overseen numerous repairs in this time.

The walls of the chapel are constructed in Carboniferous limestone with ashlar gritstone quoins. You enter the chapel through a west doorway in a porch that continues round the north side.

All the internal fittings are in the Arts and Crafts style. The barrel-vaulted plastered ceiling was designed by George Bankart, the stained glass at the east end by Louis Davis, and the altarpiece by John Cooke. Dawber designed the rood screen, and most probably also the pulpit, pews, choir stalls and light fittings.

Address St John's Road, Matlock Dale, DE4 3PQ | Getting there St John's Road is off Upperwood Road, Matlock Bath; park in Matlock Bath and walk up | Hours Contact the Friends of Friendless Churches (+44 (0) 204 520 4458) for access details | Tip St John's is close to Gulliver's Kingdom on Temple Walk, Matlock Bath (+44 (0) 1925 444888). Among the attractions are the Lost World of the Living Dinosaurs, the Dragon's Lair, a Fossil Dig and an Adventure Village.

88 St John the Baptist Parish Church

The Cathedral of the Peak

Tideswell is best known for its magnificent parish church of St John the Baptist, dubbed 'the Cathedral of the Peak'. Pevsner described St John's as 'one of the grandest of Derbyshire parish churches,' while to poet John Betjeman it was 'a grand and inspiring church'.

This stately building with its wonderfully light and airy chancel is a rarity among English parish churches in that it was almost entirely built within one period – around 70 years from 1300. This gives the elegant, Decorated-style cruciform building a wonderful uniformity that is missing from so many others. The pinnacled west tower – in the Perpendicular style – was the only later addition.

St John's is a delightfully spacious church and contains a wealth of interesting memorials, including some of the finest brasses in the Peak. These include a fine one of Bishop Robert Pursglove, who died in 1579, in full Eucharistic vestments. Pursglove was a great benefactor of the village of his birth and was the founder of Tideswell's Royal Grammar School in 1560. During the Reformation, he was one of Henry VIII's most active commissioners in the dissolution of the abbeys and monasteries.

Many of the wooden furnishings in the church, including the magnificent chancel, choir stalls and organ casing, were carved by the Hunstone family. Their firm was founded in the 19th century by brothers Robert and 'Old' Advent Hunstone. Two more generations followed, and the quality of their work is still admired today.

Although St John's does not have the dimensions of a full-blown cathedral, locals will tell you that if you measure the full length of its outside walls it would reach a mile. And Tideswell has carried on that ecclesiastical theme in the annual well dressings at its main well, which often feature 'other' British cathedrals.

Address Church Avenue, Tideswell, SK17 8LF | Getting there Tideswell is on the B6049 off the main A623 Chesterfield to Chapel-en-le-Frith road | Hours Daily 10am–4pm (except when a wedding or funeral is in progress) | Tip A short walk from Tideswell through an avenue of beech trees brings you to Tideswell Dale, which in turn leads into Miller's Dale on the River Wye. Once scarred by a group of limekilns, the valley is now a nature reserve, famous for its spring and summer flowers.

89 St Martin's Church

Worshipping in the round

Tucked away in The Nook, far from the roaring traffic of the A623, St Martin's parish church at Stoney Middleton is an unusual, very rare and quite beautiful building.

The original church, of which only the 15th-century Perpendicular tower remains, was built by local notable Joan Eyre in the 15th century in thanksgiving for the safe return of her husband, one of Shakespeare's 'band of brothers' in *Henry V,* from the Battle of Agincourt during the Hundred Years' War, in 1415. But the striking octagonal nave, one of only two in Britain – the other one is St Mary's Church at Micheldever, Hampshire – was built in 1759 following a disastrous fire which left only the tower standing.

Apparently, the revolutionary design did not immediately gain local approval, and the architect James Paine had only previously designed secular buildings, such as the stables at Chatsworth and those behind The Crescent in Buxton. Dr Charles Cox, an eminent local historian, regretted the choice of Paine as the architect and described the juxtaposition between the traditional tower and the groundbreaking octagonal design of the chancel as 'incongruous'.

The light and airy, white-walled chancel is lit by eight plain-glassed semi-circular clerestory windows in the walls above. All the pews face inwards towards the centre of the church, creating a peaceful, intimate atmosphere. The east window is the only source of colour, with beautiful stained glass installed by public subscription in 1905 on the theme of The Good Shepherd. The church was heavily restored in 1861 when the west gallery was removed, and a north vestry was added in 1880.

St Martin's has a proud record of longstanding incumbents since the reign of Elizabeth I, with the Rev Urban Smith, (1835–1887) and the Rev J. B. Riddlesden (1888–1936) successively serving the parish for over 50 years.

Address St Martin's Church, The Nook, Stoney Middleton, S32 4TZ, www.achurchnearyou.com/church/13187 | **Getting there** Just off the A623 Baslow to Tideswell road | **Hours** See website for contact details | **Tip** The Cupola café, bar, restaurant and visitor centre in The Dale, Stoney Middleton (+44 (0) 1433 627526) is a converted 18th-century lead mining cupola and a great place to recover and enjoy some locally produced food after exploring Stoney Middleton.

90 The StarDisc

A 21st-century stone circle

Following an 'extra-terrestrial vision' he had in 1997, Aidan Shingler, an artist, writer and activist (or 'reality tester' as he prefers to describe himself), sketched out an idea for a 21st-century stone circle he called a StarDisc. The name echoes that of the oldest known accurate picture of the night sky in prehistory – the Nebra Star Disc, a Bronze Age plate dated to around 1600 B.C., inlaid with gold and about the size of a vinyl LP, which was discovered in Germany in 1999. Archaeologists believe it to be an astronomical instrument with some kind of religious significance.

Shingler's objective was to create a modern, 40-foot diameter illuminated star chart carved into black granite. It would be, he claimed, a kind of radio telescope transmitting brain waves rather than radio waves, and a celestial amphitheatre that would inspire and instil wonderment. Having moved to Wirksworth in 2008, Shingler identified an ideal site for his StarDisc in the community woodland of Stoney Wood, which lies above the town. And in 2011, with Arts Council England and Lottery funding, Wirksworth's StarDisc became a reality.

The installation consists of a circle of 12 illuminated stone blocks (or seats) around a central star chart carved into black granite. It has since become a popular meeting place and venue for all kinds of community gatherings.

The opening of StarDisc in September 2011 was attended by more than a thousand people and by astronomical luminaries such as BBC *Sky at Night* presenter Pete Lawrence and co-presenter and perhaps Britain's most famous astronomer, Sir Patrick Moore. Significantly perhaps, the celebrations included an under-the-stars screening of Steven Spielberg's classic 1977 film *Close Encounters of the Third Kind*. Coincidentally, Wirksworth lies at the centre of a recent spate of UFO sightings in this part of the Peak!

Address Stoney Wood, Wirksworth, DE4 4EN | Getting there Just off the Middleton Road from Wirksworth Town Centre | Hours Accessible 24 hours | Tip The Wirksworth Heritage Centre in St John's Street, Wirksworth (+44 (0) 1629 707000) at the time of writing is closed but there are plans to re-open it. It is well worth a visit to learn more about the history of this former lead-mining township.

91 The Stepping Stones

Watch your step!

Visitors have been attracted to Dovedale and its famous Stepping Stones for well over a century, and they still come in their thousands, so it's probably a place best avoided on a sunny weekend in the summer.

A century ago, crinoline-and-bonnet-clad ladies would have been transported to the Stepping Stones by donkey, and refreshment stalls would have given sustenance to those early visitors. Today it is a National Nature Reserve in the capable hands of the National Trust and visited by over a million people annually.

Dovedale has been a honeypot ever since Charles Cotton described it as 'Princess of rivers' in his *Compleat Angler*, the fisherman's bible he wrote with Izaak Walton, which was first published in 1653 and has never been out of print since. Popularised by the Romantic movement, Dovedale's fame was further boosted by railway tourism in the early 20th century. In the 1930s, a campaign was launched to make Dovedale Britain's first National Park and it eventually became part of the Peak District National Park when it was designated in 1951.

The Stepping Stones, crossing the infant Dove in the shadow of the twin sentinels of Thorpe Cloud and Buntser Hill, are 16 limestone boulders now capped with concrete. They were set up in Victorian times to allow visitors to cross the river and explore the dale further north. Children will love the experience of skipping between the stones to cross the river but take care – when the river runs high the stones are often submerged.

When the stones were first capped by the National Trust in the early 2000s, there was a public outcry, just as there was when the trees which were obscuring the rock formations further north were felled. Unfortunately, ash dieback disease is now posing an even greater threat to Dovedale's famous ashwoods.

Address The National Trust's Dovedale car park is at DE6 2AY | Getting there The Stepping Stones are a half-mile walk from the car park | Hours Accessible 24 hours | Tip The ascent of Thorpe Cloud at the southern entrance to Dovedale is a short, steep, unrelenting climb, but well worth the effort for the bird's-eye view of the dale from the top.

92 Strip Fields

A fossilised field system

Chelmorton (locally nicknamed 'Chelly') occupies a high, shallow basin on the White Peak limestone plateau, nestling under the prominent 1,463-foot, tumulus-crowned summit of Chelmorton Low.

Chelmorton's main claim to fame, apart from being one of the highest villages in Derbyshire, is that its one main street is hemmed in by long, thin fields bordered by a network of limestone walls, which stretch far back into the surrounding countryside. These so-called strip fields belonged to the crofts or cottages that line the main street, and are often quoted by landscape historians as a classic example of medieval strip cultivation. The layout of these strip fields indicates that the village had one or possibly two medieval open fields before enclosure began in the medieval period. It is a system that is also found in villages like Monyash, Flagg and Wardlow, but Chelmorton is generally reckoned to show the finest example of this fossilised landscape.

The village was known as 'Chelmerdon' in the 12th century and is said to have derived its name from an Old English personal name and probably means 'Ceolmaer's hill'. Who was buried in the two Bronze Age barrows on top of Chelmorton Low is not known, but the view from the top extends far towards Buxton and across the White Peak plateau.

The village was founded along the banks of a little stream that goes by the charming name of Illy Willy Water. The stream provided villagers with a constant supply of pure water, which was kept in troughs, some of which still exist.

The parish church of St John the Baptist at the top of the village street has a golden locust as a weathervane on top of its 15th-century spire, recalling John's time in the wilderness. The church dates from the 11th century, and standing at 1,209 feet it is claimed to be the highest parish church in England with a spire.

Address Chelmorton, Buxton, SK17 9SL | **Getting there** Chelmorton is four and a half miles south-east of Buxton, just over a mile from the A515 Buxton to Ashbourne road | **Hours** Accessible 24 hours | **Tip** You can be sure of a cosy fire in winter, a pleasant beer garden in summer, homemade food and great guest beers all year round at The Church Inn (+44 (0) 1298 85319) at the top of the village.

93 Viator's Bridge

A bridge for a mouse

Writing in *The Compleat Angler*, Charles Cotton, the spendthrift local squire of Beresford Hall in the upper reaches of the River Dove, described the river in glowing terms: 'Oh my beloved Nymph fair Dove; Princess of rivers, how I love, Upon thy flowry banks to lye.'

Born and bred on the banks of the Dove, Cotton made the perfect guide (going under the name of Viator) to Izaak Walton (known as Piscator) in their classic fisherman's bible, one of the most successful books in the English language, first published in 1653 and never out of print since.

The popular path winding north through Dovedale leads to the tiny hamlet of Milldale, which is reached by crossing the narrow packhorse bridge known as Viator's Bridge, in reference to its celebrated appearance in *The Compleat Angler*. In it, Viator asks whether people travel in wheelbarrows hereabouts: 'Because this bridge certainly was made for nothing else; why a mouse can hardly go over it: 'Tis not two fingers broad.'

Deep in the woodlands a further three kilometres (two miles) on from Milldale in Beresford Dale is Cotton's Fishing Temple, which he built in 1674 to celebrate his friendship with Walton. Their entwined initials are carved in the stone above the door, along with the inscription *Piscatoribus Sacrum*, meaning a sacred place for anglers. There is no public access to the Fishing Temple, which lies in the grounds of Cotton's now demolished former home of Beresford Hall.

Cotton was also responsible for putting Dovedale and the Peak District on the tourist map. Apart from the best-selling *The Compleat Angler*, his 1681 English version of *The Wonders of the Peake* – a rehash of Thomas Hobbes' 1636 Latin-versed original – was one of the earliest popular guidebooks to the region. The Wonders of the Peak became a popular tourist trail for early visitors to the Peak District.

Address Viator's Bridge, Milldale, Ashbourne, DE6 2GB | Getting there Milldale is on the minor road leading west off the A515 Ashbourne to Buxton road, about four miles north of Ashbourne; car park in the village | Hours Accessible 24 hours | Tip The Fitzherbert family still occupies Tissington Hall, one of Derbyshire's most intimate manor houses, as it has for four centuries. The present house dates from the early 18th century but has been much added to over the centuries. Tissington Hall (+44 (0) 1335 352200) opens between noon and 3pm on selected dates between April and August.

94 Water-cum-Jolly Dale

Crossing the Rubicon

In what must be one of the most charmingly named spots in the country, Water-cum-Jolly Dale is a lovely hidden gem on a bend in the River Wye near Cressbrook. How it got its unusual name is a mystery, but one theory is that so-called 'jolly boats' were used in the pool below the undercut limestone crag leaning over the pool created by the millpond of nearby Cressbrook Mill. Visitors to the Victorian Tudor-style mansion of Cressbrook Hall apparently enjoyed sculling about in this beautiful setting.

Today, the usual visitors are experienced rock climbers enjoying the 40-odd routes on the beetling 65-foot Rubicon Wall dominating the tranquil pool, which is also enjoyed by anglers.

Nearby Cressbrook Mill was originally built by Richard Arkwright in 1779 for spinning cotton, and extended by William Newton in 1815. The elegant, four-storey pedimented building, complete with a lantern on the roof, is now converted to luxury flats. When it was inspected in 1807, the locally appointed inspector noted that the apprentices' rooms at Cressbrook Mill were 'clean, not crowded and apparently well conducted'.

What a contrast to Litton Mill, just upstream from Water-cum-Jolly, which was the scene, under the management of mill owner Ellis Needham, of some of the worst examples of the exploitation of child labour during the 19th century. These experiences were vividly related by Robert Blincoe – a real-life Oliver Twist who was one of the children forced to work there under appalling conditions – in the famous 1832 account entitled *A Memoir of Robert Blincoe*, written by a Lancashire writer named John Brown. Brown described Blincoe as 'a moral outcast', and his book was the first time the story of a working-class factory worker had been described. The book was instrumental in the eventual changing of the law concerning child labour, when the Ten Hours Bill was passed in 1847.

Address Water-cum-Jolly Dale is near Cressbrook, SK17 8SX, what3words: lizard.obviously.search | Getting there A short walk down to the river and Water-cum-Jolly Dale from the village of Cressbrook | Hours Accessible 24 hours | Tip Cressbrook Hall (+44 (0) 1298 871289), situated high on the northern bank of the Wye, is a Tudor-style mansion built by the Cressbrook Mill owner William McConnel in 1835, and now used as a wedding venue.

95 Waterfall Swallet

A hidden gem

The Peak District can boast most landforms apart from a coastline, but the one it is not so blessed with is large waterfalls. The best known is probably the 100-foot Kinder Downfall on the western edge of Kinder Scout, which has the uncanny habit of flowing back uphill in stormy weather, and Panniers Pool at Three Shires Head. And there is a series of pretty rowan-fringed falls in the Black Cloughs of Longdendale and some equally delightful ones in the Alport Valley on the southern slopes of Bleaklow.

But in the limestone dales of the White Peak, waterfalls are singularly absent. So, what a delight to discover Waterfall Swallet, just off the road between Eyam and Foolow, a delightful 60-foot waterfall, where a stream flowing off Eyam Edge cascades in dancing curtains of spray into a dramatic and secret wooded amphitheatre.

A swallet, swallow or shakehole is a natural depression which takes a stream underground in porous limestone country, usually creating caves beneath, and several caves have been explored by local cavers beneath the Waterfall Swallet. But the cavers' guide warns that 'rescue would be almost impossible through the tight entrance passages'.

Access to the swallet is not easy, so it should not be attempted by anyone uncertain of their footing. It involves a steep climb down a slippery wooded bank which is strewn with the branches of fallen trees.

But once you get there, the atmosphere in the wooded amphitheatre is truly magical. The only sound is that of the cascading water as it tumbles down the striated strata of the cliff face, creating a shimmering curtain of spray. And as with any waterfall, the best effects will be obtained after heavy rainfall – which incidentally will make your path down to the swallet even more treacherous, so take extra care.

Address Waterfall Swallet, near Foolow, S32 5QA | Getting there Just off the Eyam to Foolow road, about two miles from Eyam; limited parking on site | Hours Accessible 24 hours but safer in daylight | Tip The waterfall is close to the hamlet of Foolow which, in turn, is adjacent to the dry valley of Silly Dale. The names have nothing to do with the intelligence of the locals! Foolow means 'multi-coloured hill' and Silly Dale, simply means 'happy dale'.

96_Well Dressings

Unique examples of folk art

The well dressings of the Peak District are unique examples of folk art. They attract thousands of visitors to local villages throughout the summer, who come to marvel at their intricate and colourful designs, each one different from the other and all created by villagers usually using purely natural, locally found materials.

Originally created only in the villages of the White Peak, they now take place in over 80 towns and villages in and around the Peak District. Throughout the summer, each village takes it in turn to decorate their wells or springs with these intricate floral icons, which often coincide with the village Wakes (patron saints) Week.

It is thought that the custom originated in Pagan times as a thanksgiving for the gift of water on the fast-draining limestone plateau, but the custom was later adopted by Christianity, and the pretty Fitzherbert estate village of Tissington is generally regarded as the birthplace of the tradition in its modern form.

The earliest reference to where the custom began was at Tissington in 1348/9, as a thanksgiving when the village escaped the deadly infestation of the Black Death, or Bubonic Plague, which had ravished the Derbyshire countryside.

For many visitors, Tissington is the perfect White Peak village, especially at Ascension tide in May when the five beautiful well dressings – traditionally the first and earliest-recorded in the Peak – are put in place. The wells, or springs, in Tissington are the Yew Tree, Hall, Hands, Coffin, Town Wells and the later addition of a Children's Well, which usually attracts the most attention.

Well dressing is a real community effort, and villagers from all walks of life are involved in the process of creating the beautiful floral mosaic icons, which are created by pressing petals into soft clay held within a wooden frame. A well dressing can take up to 400 hours to complete, but it only lasts for a week.

Address Tissington, Ashbourne, DE6 1RA, www.facebook.com/TissingtonWellDressings | **Getting there** Tissington is off the A515 Buxton to Ashbourne road | **Hours** See the Facebook page for details of the annual event | **Tip** The sturdy Norman tower of the parish church of St Mary watches over the village green at Tissington, and is well worth a visit. Look out for the 1643 Fitzherbert monument, featuring ladies in Jacobean dress.

97 Wheston Cross

A rare wayside monument

The finely carved Wheston Cross, standing in a sheltering copse of trees opposite Bottom Farm at Wheston, a mile west of Tideswell, is a rare survival of a preaching cross. Dating from the 14th or 15th centuries, it marked the way from Tideswell to Buxton on the Forest Road leading through the medieval Royal (hunting) Forest of the Peak, which once covered an area of 180 square miles of the northern Peak.

There were once thought to be as many as 12,000 medieval standing crosses in England, but only about 2,000 survive today. The crosses served a variety of purposes, in villages as places for preaching, public proclamations and penance, and in the countryside to mark boundaries between parishes, property or settlements. Wheston Cross was moved to its present site earlier this century from the centre of the village close to Wheston Hall.

The cross stands 11 feet high on two steps and the cusped and decorated cross-head incorporates on its west face a figure of the Virgin and Child, with a star over the Virgin's head and sunbursts at the ends of the cross-arms. On the east face is the crucified torso of Christ, arms spread wide but lacking many facial features.

Wheston was known in the 18th century as Whetstone and was recorded in the Domesday Book as an outlier of Hope under the King's manor of Tideswell. Wheston Hall (private) was originally built in the late 16th century, and was held by the Alleyne family, who were staunch Roman Catholics. In 1592 Edward Alleyne and his brother Henry were arrested for being Catholics and for holding secret masses, and were heavily fined.

The road on which Wheston Cross stands leads down Wheston Bank and was formerly known as Kirkgate or Crossgate. This era of the Middle Ages is sometimes referred to as the Age of Faith, and no traveller would have passed a cross without offering a prayer for their continued safe journey.

Address Wheston, nr. Tideswell, Buxton, SK17 8JB | Getting there About a mile west of Tideswell on a minor road leading towards Peak Forest | Hours Accessible 24 hours | Tip The hamlet of Wheston gets its name from the whetstones which were formerly manufactured there to sharpen blades.

98 Windy Knoll Cave

An Ice Age cemetery

It's hard to imagine it today, but mammoths, rhinoceros, bison, reindeer, hyena, lions, bears and wolves once roamed the lush limestone uplands above Castleton at the end of the last Ice Age. The fossilised remains of all these exotic animals were found by antiquaries excavating Windy Knoll Cave in the late 19th century.

Dating from the late Pleistocene (Ice Age) period of about 30,000 years ago, the remains were thought to have accumulated when herds of mammoth, bison and reindeer on migration through the nearby Winnats Pass to avoid the encroaching icefields somehow fell, or were chased, into the fissure. The carnivores, such as the wolves, lions and bears, must have tracked the bison and reindeer on their annual migrations. A radiocarbon date of about 37,300 years was obtained on a bison bone from the cave in 1996.

The fissure in which the bones were discovered is now filled in, and the remains are kept at the British Museum in London and at museums in Manchester, Derby, Cambridge and the now sadly closed Buxton Museum.

The gaping, grass-topped cave, now fenced off with 'Keep Out' signs, is adjacent to a quarry at Windy Knoll which has revealed small quantities of a rare, sticky-brown hydrocarbon mineral known as elaterite, similar to that found in the tar lakes of Trinidad. The distinctive colouration of the Blue John, a semi-precious mineral, may have been caused by these hydrocarbons in the groundwater, but please note that the site is strictly protected as an SSSI.

The large entrance chamber of Windy Knoll Cave narrows and dips further back for 40 yards, where it is blocked by a boulder choke. The 1874 and 1876 excavations by Sir William Boyd Dawkins and Rooke Pennington of some nine cubic yards of cave deposits produced an astonishing haul of 6,800 animal bones, including bison, reindeer, bear and wolves.

Address Windy Knoll Cave, Castleton, High Peak | Getting there Signposted off the A625 Castleton to Chapel-en-le-Frith road, a couple of miles outside Castleton | Hours Accessible 24 hours | Tip It's a short, if steep, climb up from Windy Knoll to the 1,696-foot summit of Mam Tor, Castleton's 'Mother Mountain', which offers outstanding views of the Kinder Scout plateau to the north and the rolling hills of the White Peak to the south.

99 The Winnats Pass

The murder of Allan and Clara

This spectacular limestone gorge west of Castleton rivals the better-known Cheddar Gorge in Somerset for the drama of its scenery. Formed as a result of underwater currents when this part of the White Peak was a shallow, tropical sea some 350 million years ago, since the collapse of the Mam Tor road it now carries the main A625 road to Chapel-en-le-Frith.

But this well-known beauty spot harbours a deadly secret. In 1758 it was the scene of the tragic robbing and murder of a couple named Allan and Clara, who were eloping to be married at the church of King Charles the Martyr at Peak Forest. Accused but never charged were a group of local lead miners, all of whom met gruesome deaths themselves in later years.

One fell to his death from a buttress and another was killed by a falling rock, both in the pass; the third committed suicide and the fourth went mad. The fifth eventually confessed to the dreadful crime on his deathbed. The bodies of Allan and Clara were eventually discovered 10 years after the event by some miners who were sinking an engine pit in a mine shaft close to the pass.

Memories are long in this part of the world, so a melodramatic account of this 'brutal and horrible' murder, written by an anonymous local person sometime in the 1930s, declined to name the guilty miners for fear of upsetting their living families, using just the initials of their surnames instead. The saddle said to be from Clara's horse is kept in the village museum, now housed in the Castleton National Park Visitor Centre.

The Winnats and nearby Treak Cliff are also the source of one of the few remaining sources of the rare semi-precious mineral known as Blue John, a rare form of fluorite with purple-blue or yellow banding. The name comes from the French words for blue and yellow, and the mineral is still worked into jewellery and other items in local shops.

Address Castleton, Hope Valley, S33 8WA | Getting there The Winnats Pass is about a mile west of Castleton on the main A625 road to Chapel-en-le-Frith | Hours Accessible 24 hours | Tip A tiny plaque in the grassy sward of The Winnats Pass commemorates G. H. B. Ward, the Sheffield rambler who was a regular speaker at the annual access rallies held here during the 1930s.

100 Winster Market House

First National Trust property in the Peak

The National Trust, which cares for 12 per cent of the Peak District National Park, is the largest single landowner in the 555-square-mile area, owning 67 square miles. But Winster Market House, the charity's first property in the Peak District and one of its first nationally, was acquired as early as 1906 for the princely sum of £50.

The two-storey, coursed stone-based, red-brick Market House has five, once open but now infilled, arches and stands four-square in the centre of the main street of the pretty White Peak village. It is thought to date from the 16th century, when it formed the centrepiece of the original prosperous market town, granted its charter in the 17th century. Annual cattle markets were regularly held before the First World War, when sheep were herded along Pump Lane, and cattle and horses were sold in front of the Miner's Standard public house.

The building was commissioned by the Lords of the Manor, who in 1570 were Gervase and Anthony Eyre of Newbold Manor. It was designed in the neoclassical style, and originally open on the ground floor where the markets were held, with an assembly hall on the first floor.

The arches were infilled with coursed stone, probably in the first half of the 19th century, to encourage alternative use, but the use of the building for the sale of agricultural goods declined significantly in the wake of the decline in the lead mining industry and in British agriculture in the late 19th century. The building fell vacant and its condition deteriorated. The upper storey had to be removed for safety in 1904. But eventually it was acquired by the National Trust in 1906.

The first floor was restored and the assembly room subsequently fitted with interpretation panels describing the history of Winster and its importance in the local lead mining industry.

Address Winster Market House, Main Street, Winster, DE4 2DJ, www.nationaltrust.org.uk/visit/peak-district-derbyshire/winster-market-house | Getting there About five miles south of Bakewell on the B5056 | Hours Check website for opening times | Tip Winster's famous Morris dancers (www.winstermorrisdancers.org) were founded in 1863 and perform the 15 dances in the Winster tradition, including The Winster Gallop.

101 Climbing a 'Weird' Matterhorn

Shutlingsloe's secret stone

A landmark for miles around and dubbed 'the Matterhorn of Cheshire', Shutlingsloe is a distinctively conical, 1,660-foot hill above the village of Wildboarclough on the western edge of the Peak District National Park.

But it is probably best known as the site of the dénouement of Alan Garner's classic children's fantasy novel *The Weirdstone of Brisingamen*, first published in 1960 and still thrilling young readers today. Garner, who still lives locally, frequently used the landscape of the Cheshire Peak and Alderley Edge in his stories.

In the climax of the Weirdstone story, a great battle of the forces of good against the forces of evil takes place on 'Shuttlingslow', where a group of children and their companions make a desperate last stand to protect the Weirdstone, a magical, tear-shaped jewel held in a bracelet. Eventually, the forces of good prevail and the power of the Weirdstone is used to subdue the forces of darkness.

The name of Shutlingsloe derives from the Old English 'Scyttel's hlaw', meaning 'Scyttel's hill', named after an otherwise unknown Saxon. Geologically speaking, the hill is formed from layers of mudstones and coarse gritstones laid down in a delta during the Carboniferous period, some 350 million years ago. The rocky summit tor commands excellent views west over the Cheshire Plain towards the outskirts of Manchester, to airliners arriving and departing from Manchester Airport, the white saucer of the Jodrell Bank radio telescope and, on a clear day, as far as the Mersey Estuary and the Clwydian Hills of Wales, 40 miles away.

Shutlingsloe, which despite its nickname is actually only the third highest hill in Cheshire, is easily reached by a short, partly paved but finally steep footpath from the village of Wildboarclough.

Start/end point The village of Wildboarclough, SK11 0BD | Distance About three miles | Map OS 1:25,000 Explorer OL24 The Peak District, White Peak Area | Best time to visit Any time of the year, but winter should be avoided unless you are equipped for snow and/or icy conditions | Difficulty Shutlingsloe is easily reached by a short, partly paved but finally steep footpath from the village of Wildboarclough. This is a moorland walk – wear boots and waterproofs | Tip The Crag Inn on Nabbs Road, Wildboarclough, SK11 0BD (+44 (0) 1260 227239) was originally a farm built in 1629 and was converted to a beer house in 1825. Known as 'Bottom of the Hill', it's at the foot of the footpath to Shutlingsloe, so is ideal for after-climb refreshment.

102 Crossing a Bridge Too Far

Slippery Stones transplanted bridge

The twin-arched, parapeted packhorse bridge at Slippery Stones, above the Howden Dam in the Upper Derwent Valley, has a peripatetic history. It was originally sited four miles downstream in Derwent village, before the village was depopulated to make way for the Ladybower Reservoir in the 1930s. Originally built in the Middle Ages, the bridge had stood opposite Derwent Hall on the Sheffield to Derwent packhorse route.

When work began on the construction of the Ladybower Dam, the bridge was dismantled and the stones carefully numbered and kept in storage in a barn for 20 years. Then in 1959 it was re-erected on the site of another former packhorse bridge at Slippery Stones, above the string of Upper Derwent Valley reservoirs.

The restored bridge was dedicated to the memory of John Derry, a prominent Sheffield journalist and access campaigner, who explained the name of the site of the former bridge in *Across the Derbyshire Moors*: 'You... have to ford the stream as best you may, and if you have no nails in your shoes you understand why the stones have annexed the adjective "slippery".'

The pools in the infant River Derwent above and below the Slippery Stones bridge have become very popular with picnickers and wild swimmers, and the track, known as Cut Gate, leads up the bank opposite, linking the Upper Derwent with Langsett and the Upper Don across the Howden and Midhope Moors. The Cut Gate Track was first recorded in 1561, when it was described as 'Cartgate', so it may have been used by small, horse-drawn carts taking produce from the Upper Derwent to Penistone market.

Much excellent restoration work has been undertaken in the area by the National Trust and the Moors for the Future partnership.

Start/end point Limited parking in the layby at the end of the road along the western shoreline of Howden Reservoir, where a forestry track leads to Slippery Stones | Distance If the road is closed, you will have to park at the Fairholmes Visitor Centre (S33 0AQ) and walk the five miles alongside the reservoir to reach Slippery Stones | Map OS 1:25,000 Explorer OL1 The Peak District, Dark Peak Area | Best time to visit Any time of the year | Difficulty Easy walking on minor roads and forest tracks | Tip At the end of the metalled road as you approach Slippery Stones you come to the small roundabout known as King's Tree or Royal Oak. The tree was planted by King George VI in September 1945, when he opened the Ladybower Reservoir with Queen Elizabeth.

103 Crossroads of Counties

Where Three Shires meet

An ever-popular subject for calendars and postcards, Three Shires Head on Axe Edge Moor is where the counties of Cheshire, Derbyshire and Staffordshire meet at a picturesque packhorse bridge over the River Dane.

Once the scene of illicit bare-knuckle prize fights – the fighters would step from one county to another to avoid arrest if the police arrived – this is a pleasant two-mile walk from the pretty village of Wildboarclough in Cheshire.

The presence of the single-arched, 18th-century packhorse bridge indicates the former importance of the route for traders crossing the moors between Buxton, Macclesfield and Congleton. Silk thread produced at nearby Hollinsclough and Flash was regularly sent by packhorse to the silk manufacturing town of Macclesfield. In the 17th century, coal was also sent by packhorse, from the shallow workings on Axe Edge to the towns on the Cheshire plain.

Below the bridge is a series of pretty waterfalls and pools, which have become popular with wild swimmers, although be warned, the pools can be icy cold. The main pool can be up to seven feet deep, but the depth varies depending on the time of year.

Our walk begins from the Clough House car park in Wildboarclough and goes over fields to cross a small wooden bridge over Cumberland Brook. The path goes through a series of gates to a signpost marked 'Flash via Three Shires Head'. You then have to carefully cross the busy A54 Buxton to Congleton road by a gate and follow a fingerpost down a series of metal steps across a field through two metal kissing gates to follow the wall that takes you down to the footpath to the River Dane.

You are now on the Dane Valley Way, which leads you to the packhorse bridge at Three Shires Head. Retrace your steps to return to the village of Wildboarclough.

Start/end point Clough House car park, Wildboarclough, SK11 0BD | Distance 2.2 miles | Map OS 1:25,000 Explorer OL24 The Peak District, White Peak Area | Best time to visit Late summer or early autumn is a good time to visit Three Shires Head – the surrounding moors are purple with heather | Difficulty Mostly field walking but with a few rocky sections and steps; wear boots and waterproofs | Tip Wildboarclough was once famous for having the grandest Post Office in England, which was housed in the three-storeyed Crag Mill, the administrative block for a former silk mill (now private).

104 The 'Eleven a.m. Rock'

Dovedale's unwitting timepiece

It's an apocryphal tale, but one there is every reason to suppose is true. An information assistant in the Bakewell Visitor Centre was approached by a puzzled-looking visitor. The ever-helpful assistant asked if she could help. The visitor replied: 'I've been up and down the dale and I just can't find it.' 'What can't you find?' enquired the assistant. 'This eleven a.m. rock,' she said.

To understand her quandary, you have to imagine the word 'Ilam' written in hand-scripted text, as it was in Mark Richards' popular walking guide to the *White Peak Dales*. It *does* look like 11am. To her eternal credit, the witty assistant responded: 'Well, what time of the day were you there?'

Ilam Rock is a slender, 82-foot leaning spire of Carboniferous reef limestone on the Staffordshire bank of the River Dove. It is made up of the fossilised remains of sea creatures and corals, and its verticality has attracted rock climbers for over a century.

Although there are rumours of a local quarryman climbing the rock 50 years before by using spikes driven into cracks, the first recorded ascent was by Samuel Turner in 1903. Watched by hundreds of cheering spectators, Turner made the climb by throwing a rope over the summit and then clambering up, 'hand-over-hand like an acrobat', to reach the top.

The first recognised rock climb known as the Original Route was by Siegfried Herford, one of the top climbers of the day, who was to be killed at Ypres less than two years later, in August 1914, in the bloodiest battle of the First World War. The most popular of the seven aid-assisted routes on Ilam Rock today is Easter Island, graded E2 in the climbers' guide and simply described as 'sensational'. It was first climbed by Ed Ward-Drummond in 1972.

Start / end point Milldale car park, Milldale, Ashbourne, DE6 2GB | Distance Ilam Rock is an easy, three-mile walk from the National Trust car park at Milldale, passing Ravens Tor and the gaping caves of Dove Holes | Map OS 1:25,000 Explorer OL24 The Peak District, White Peak Area | Best time to visit Any time of the year, but best to avoid a busy summer Bank Holiday or weekend | Difficulty An easy, level riverside path with just one or two stiles to cross | Tip The adventurous might like to climb up to the shallow cave that gapes at the foot of Pickering Tor, another towering spire of reef limestone that stands on the opposite Derbyshire bank of the Dove.

105 In the Footsteps of a God

The mystery of Carl Wark

Once described as 'an immense blackened altar populated by Druids', the enigmatic enclosure known as Carl Wark on the moors above Hathersage has puzzled archaeologists for years.

Usually described as an Iron Age hillfort, the 1.7-acre enclosure on a gritstone promontory is defended by natural crags that have been enhanced by a massive, 130-foot-long, 10-foot-high drystone wall on its western rampart. Described as being 'unlike any other structure found in Northern England', this Cyclopean defensive wall comprises eight courses of stone, the largest of which is five feet long by two feet wide.

No evidence of settlement has been found within the enclosure, and it is thought it may have been used as a place of refuge for the local population, or it may have had some ceremonial or ritual purpose. More recent archaeological thinking suggests that the site may even have been in use since the Neolithic period, with multiple uses and phases of construction.

The origin of the name Carl Wark is as mysterious as its age. Variously recorded as 'Cair's Work' or 'Chair' and 'Carleswark', it has been suggested that the name is Old Norse in origin, meaning 'The Old Man's Fort' – the Old Man referring to the Norse god Odin or the Devil. Danish settlers in the area in the 9th to 10th centuries may have regarded the enclosure as suspiciously sinister, ancient and mysterious. But the name could equally well have derived from the Welsh word *caer*, meaning fort or rampart, and there is a large, overhanging boulder to the north of the enclosure which is named Caer's Chair.

Whatever the truth, Carl Wark still possesses what archaeologist Edward Trustram described in 1911 as 'a wild grandeur and solemn dignity not often witnessed in England'.

Start / end point The National Trust's Longshaw car park at S11 7TZ | Distance Carl Wark is just over two miles' walk from the car park; cross the A625 Sheffield road, with care, then use the Duke's Road footpath and cross the Burbage Brook by the packhorse bridge | Map OS 1:25,000 Explorer OL1 The Peak District, Dark Peak Area | Best time to visit Late summer, when the heather is in full bloom on Hathersage Moor | Difficulty Moorland walking on stony paths, so good footwear essential | Tip Carl Wark was used as a location in the popular 1987 film *The Princess Bride,* with the dominant Higger Tor prominent in the background.

106 The Mermaid Walk

The legend of Doxey Pool

For a place that is about as far from the sea as you can get in the British Isles, the Peak District is home to several pools which curiously have attracted legends involving mermaids. There's the Mermaid's Pool under the southern escarpment of Kinder Scout, and Blakemere Pool at Morridge in the Staffordshire Moorlands.

And almost within sight of Blakemere Pool is perhaps the most famous of the Peak's mermaid pools. Doxey Pool is a dark, rock-rimmed tarn on the high ridge of The Roaches, which always seems to keep its level while having no visible source of supply. According to legend, the pool is bottomless, and home to a sinister mermaid known as Jenny Greenteeth.

The story of an encounter a local woman had with Jenny in 1949 lends credence to the legend. Florence Pettit was looking forward to an early morning wild swim in Doxey Pool. But while she prepared for her swim, she watched horrified as a monstrous, green, dripping, weed-clad creature rose 30 feet from the waters of the pool. It gave her a menacing stare before sinking back beneath the dark waters from whence it came.

The origin of the Jenny Greenteeth legend is lost in the mists of time, although local folklore suggests that the mermaid is the spirit of an unfortunate woman who drowned in the pool and now lies in wait for the unwary walker, to drag them to a similar fate.

Jenny Greenteeth is a well-known regional name for a wizened hag with green skin, long hair and sharp teeth. But the word Doxey is also an old name for a prostitute or a sexually promiscuous woman and is sometimes linked to the Celtic goddess of fertility, Brigid. No one really knows, but until recently, flowers were regularly left by a boulder on the now-fenced shores of Doxey Pool, perhaps in tribute to Brigid – or Jenny? The mystery of Britain's most land-locked mermaid remains.

Start / end point Roadside parking near Rockhall Cottage, ST13 8UA | Distance Doxey Pool lies at the southern end of The Roaches ridge, accessed via a moorland footpath of about a mile from Rockhall Cottage | Map OS 1:25,000 Explorer OL24 The Peak District, White Peak Area | Best time to visit Late summer when the heather on The Roaches ridge is in full bloom | Difficulty This is a serious moorland walk – wear boots and waterproofs | Tip The award-winning Roaches Tea Room and Restaurant on Roach Road, Upper Hulme (ST13 8TY), offers fine, homemade meals with breathtaking views over Tittesworth reservoir and as far as the Welsh mountains.

107 On the Trail of the Green Knight

To Lud's hidden church

The first visit to Lud's Church, a huge landslip hidden deep among the trees of Back Forest above the remote valley of the Black Brook in the Staffordshire Moorlands, is an eerie experience. It is a secret, secluded place which exudes mystery and menace.

To the walker who enters this strange roofless cavern, the overall impression is one of dark, dank and dripping greenness. Grass, moss and ferns hang from the sides of the 100-foot-long ravine which, camouflaged by trees, is almost invisible from above.

It's the perfect place to attract myths and legends. Lud's Church is thought to take its name from Walter de Ludank, a Lollard follower of John Wycliffe during the Reformation, who held illicit services in the remote spot, far from the prying eyes of the authorities.

But the most persistent legend about Lud's Church is that it was the setting for that masterpiece of medieval alliterative poetry, *Sir Gawain and the Green Knight*. This work has been hailed as the greatest medieval poem outside the work of Chaucer.

All that can be said with certainty about the author is that language experts who have studied the text have said that the dialect used places him unmistakeably in the northwest Midlands, or the Staffordshire part of the Peak District. And the beheading ritual undertaken by Sir Gawain with the mysterious Green Knight of the gruesome Arthurian tale takes place in 'the Green Chapel', which has been closely identified with Lud's Church and the surrounding countryside.

Our walk follows the road north beneath The Roaches and Five Clouds for one mile to Roach End, where you turn left over a stile (signposted) to descend through heather into Forest Wood and Back Forest. Follow the clear path to a clearing where Lud's Church is signposted. Return via the same route.

Start / end point Limited parking near Rockhall Cottage on Roaches Road, ST13 8UA, so it's best to get there early; The Roaches road is just west of the A53 Buxton to Leek road | Distance About 3 miles | Map OS 1:25,000 Explorer OL24 The Peak District, White Peak Area | Best time to visit Try to avoid a summer weekend, when The Roaches are very popular, especially with rock climbers | Difficulty An easy road walk, then forest tracks leading to Lud's Church | Tip You can combine a visit to Lud's Church with an exploration of the nearby rocky outcrops of The Roaches, Hen Cloud and Ramshaw Rocks, favourite spots for rock climbers.

108 A 'Reforming' Walk

Earl Grey's Tower

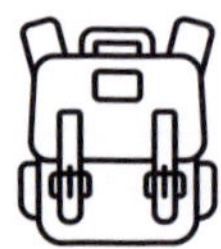

Stanton Moor is an isolated, heather-clad gritstone outlier overlooking the Derwent Valley. Apart from its wealth of prehistoric remains – it was described by H. J. Massingham as 'as thick with tumuli as a plumduff with raisons' – one of its most prominent features, especially when viewed from the A6, is the Earl Grey, or Reform, Tower on its eastern edge.

Most people will probably associate Earl Grey with the aromatic, bergamot-flavoured tea, which may have been named after Charles, 2nd Earl Grey, Whig Prime Minister from 1830 to 1834. But Earl Grey was also well known for being the driving force behind the 1832 Reform Bill, which did away with the so-called 'rotten boroughs' – sparsely populated Parliamentary constituencies that had previously elected several MPs. Also under his leadership, slavery was abolished throughout the British Empire in 1833.

The Earl Grey Tower on Stanton Moor (it's windowless, so is known by some as 'Rapunzel's Tower') was built around 1833 by William Pole Thornhill of nearby Stanton Hall to commemorate the passing of the Reform Act. It is claimed that Thornhill strongly supported Parliamentary reform and deliberately built the tower so that it could be visible from Haddon Hall, the property of the 5th Duke of Rutland, a diehard Tory who opposed the Act.

The doorway on the east face is now blocked off, but until the 1950s, a staircase allowed visitors to see the spectacular view from the roof of the tower. A niche above the doorway originally had a plaque with a coronet and the inscription 'Earl Grey 1832'.

As Massingham observed, Stanton Moor had long been a sacred space to our prehistoric forebears. Chief among the many monuments found there is the Bronze Age Nine Ladies Stone Circle and associated King Stone, set within an atmospheric amphitheatre of spindly birch trees.

Start / end point Park on the minor road (off the B5056) between Birchover and Rowsley | Distance A one-mile walk along the eastern edge of Stanton Moor to reach the tower | Best time to visit As with any moorland situation, late summer to early autumn is the best time to appreciate the blooming heather | Difficulty This is a moorland walk – wear boots and waterproofs | Tip The Druid's Inn at the end of nearby Birchover's Main Street (+44 (0) 1629 650424) has served villagers since 1851 and takes its name from the supposed (but mistaken) Druidical connections with the cave-ridden Rowtor Rocks, just behind the pub.

109 Rock with the Caveman

Thor's Cave still yawns

Thor's Cave yawns menacingly, high above Staffordshire's Manifold Valley near the hilltop village of Wetton, looking exactly like the archetypal cartoon caveman's dwelling. You half expect to see Fred Flintstone emerging from its inky depths, shouting 'Wilma!' at the top of his voice.

In the late 19th century, excavations led by the Rev G. H. Wilson, removed nearly two tons of earth from Thor's and the nearby Thor's Fissure cave. Their finds included the remains of at least seven people dating from the prehistoric period, as well as Romano-British jewellery. More recent digs have revealed even earlier (Palaeolithic) material – so maybe Fred and Wilma lived there after all.

Geologically speaking, the crag in which Thor's Cave is situated is a classic example of an outcrop of reef limestone dating from the Carboniferous period around 350 million years ago, when this part of the Peak was basking under a tropical sea close to the Equator. Blanketed by an immense glacier during the last Ice Age, the infant Manifold channelled its meltwaters and carved out the valley around these harder, upstanding reefs, leaving them as the isolated crags we see today.

There has long been a debate over the name of Thor's Cave, and many guidebooks still link it to the eponymous hammer-wielding Norse God of thunder. Modern etymologists, however, believe that it comes from the Old English *torr*, which simply means a high rock or a rocky hill.

As the Rev Wilson wrote nearly a century ago: 'This great cave… supplies an appropriate stage for any uncanny phantom which a vivid imagination can conjure up… Sitting at the cave mouth after watching a gorgeous sunset die out over the distant hills, the deepening gloom seemed to recreate an atmosphere full of the things of a misty, forgotten past.'

Start / end point You can reach Thor's Cave by a series of steep, sometimes slippery, steps direct from the Manifold Way walking and cycling route, or from the free car park in Carr Lane, Wetton, DE6 2AF | Distance From Wetton, it's a 5.5 mile walk along a signposted concession track and footpath, or from the Manifold Track, a steep, half-mile climb | Map OS 1:25,000 Explorer OL24 The Peak District, White Peak Area | Best time to visit Any time of the year, but the rocks of Thor's Cave can be slippery when wet | Difficulty Easy field paths from Wetton, but a steep climb from the Manifold Track | Tip The Royal Oak pub on the village green at Wetton (+44 (0) 1335 31028), sheltering under its eponymous tree, is renowned as a walkers' pub, and is also family and dog friendly.

110 To a Stone Age Viewpoint

Taddington's tumulus

Standing at just under 1,400 feet, like a massive broken tooth above the A6 Bakewell to Buxton road, the Five Wells Neolithic chambered cairn above the village of Taddington is claimed to be one of the highest such monuments in the country.

Three large, lichen-covered stones mark the main entrance to the paved main chamber of the scheduled ancient monument, which has been dramatically reduced in size by local farmers over the years. A second, even less well-preserved chamber stands to the west.

The burial mound which once covered it was over 66 feet in diameter and was originally excavated by the prolific local barrow-digger Thomas Bateman in 1846. Bateman discovered the remains of at least twelve human skeletons, and five more have since been discovered by modern archaeologists. Subsequent excavations, by Llewellyn Jewitt, William Lukis and Micah Salt, have also found distinctive Neolithic pottery and flint tools in the chambers and passages, and a separate cist (stone coffin) within the cairn.

It is thought that originally there were two entrances, and that visitors had to crawl in on their hands and knees to reach the back chambers in the dark heart of the mound. Modern archaeologists have suggested that the bones of the ancestors were regularly removed when required for seasonal rites and ceremonies. It's somehow good to learn that no one really knows.

The site enjoys fine views north across the Wye Valley and the deep defile of Chee Dale towards the hills beyond, so the lofty location and extensive views must have been significant to its Neolithic builders some 5,000 years ago. It's touching to think that the cairn was built originally so that the ancestors could watch over their descendants.

Start/end point Access is by foot only, via a signed permitted path from Pillwell Gate to the west or from the Limestone Way long-distance footpath, which runs along Sough Lane 550 yards to the east | Distance About half a mile from Pillwell Gate, or a mile from Sough Lane | Map OS 1:25,000 Explorer OL24 The Peak District, White Peak Area | Best time to visit Any time of the year | Difficulty An easy ascent along lanes and field paths | Tip The Queen's Arms in Taddington's Main Street (+44 (0) 1298 85447) is a friendly local offering hearty meat pies, steaks and a fine pint of beer. The tasty Yorkshire pudding is especially recommended.

111 Watch a River Reappear

A Lathkill Dale wonder

It's one of the usually unseen but most spectacular natural wonders of the Peak District, only seen in winter or after heavy rain. It is the explosive re-emergence of the River Lathkill from the cave of its birth at the head of Lathkill Dale, near Monyash. The waters gush out of the shallow, fern-draped cave entrance with frightening force, rushing downstream in several channels to join the normal course of the river.

The Lathkill is a rarity in Britain. It is a disappearing river that rises and runs for the whole of its length on Carboniferous limestone, which also makes it one of the cleanest and purest rivers in the country. Three hundred years ago, Charles Cotton was moved to describe it in *The Compleat Angler* as the purest and most transparent stream he ever saw, at home or abroad. According to Cotton, it also bred 'the reddest, and the best Trouts in England'.

But the Lathkill mysteriously disappears underground in sinkholes during dry spells and for most of the summer, which makes its winter reappearance – technically known as a resurgence – that much more exciting.

The wide cave entrance gives access to 984 yards of passages (one chamber is named 'Lathkiller Hall'), which have been explored by experienced cavers. But the whole system floods in wet weather, and mere mortals should not be tempted to explore any further than the cave entrance.

Just upstream from Lathkill Head Cave on the way from Monyash, where the dale narrows to a slender defile through the rocks, are the extensive spoil heaps from the former Ricklow Quarry. The northern face of the quarry contains large numbers of *Gigantoproductus* fossils stacked on top of each other. The fossil-rich rock was quarried here in Victorian times and polished to create decorative items.

Start/end point Limited parking by the road as you approach Monyash on the B5055 from Bakewell at the head of Lathkill Dale | Map OS 1:25,000 Explorer OL24 The Peak District, White Peak Area | Distance Two miles, with some rocky stiles, to Lathkill Head Cave; wear sturdy footwear | Best time to visit In the spring or early summer you will be rewarded with Lathkill Dale's glorious profusion of wildflowers, including orchids and rock rose. But most precious of all is the stand of rare, purple-flowered Jacob's Ladder where the path narrows to a gorge just past Ricklow Quarry | Tip The threshold of The Bull's Head in Church Street, Monyash, DE45 1JH (+44 (0) 1629 812372), is a panel of 350-million-year-old crinoid fossils, evidence of the immense geological history of the area. You are likely to join locals supping pints in this traditional country pub.

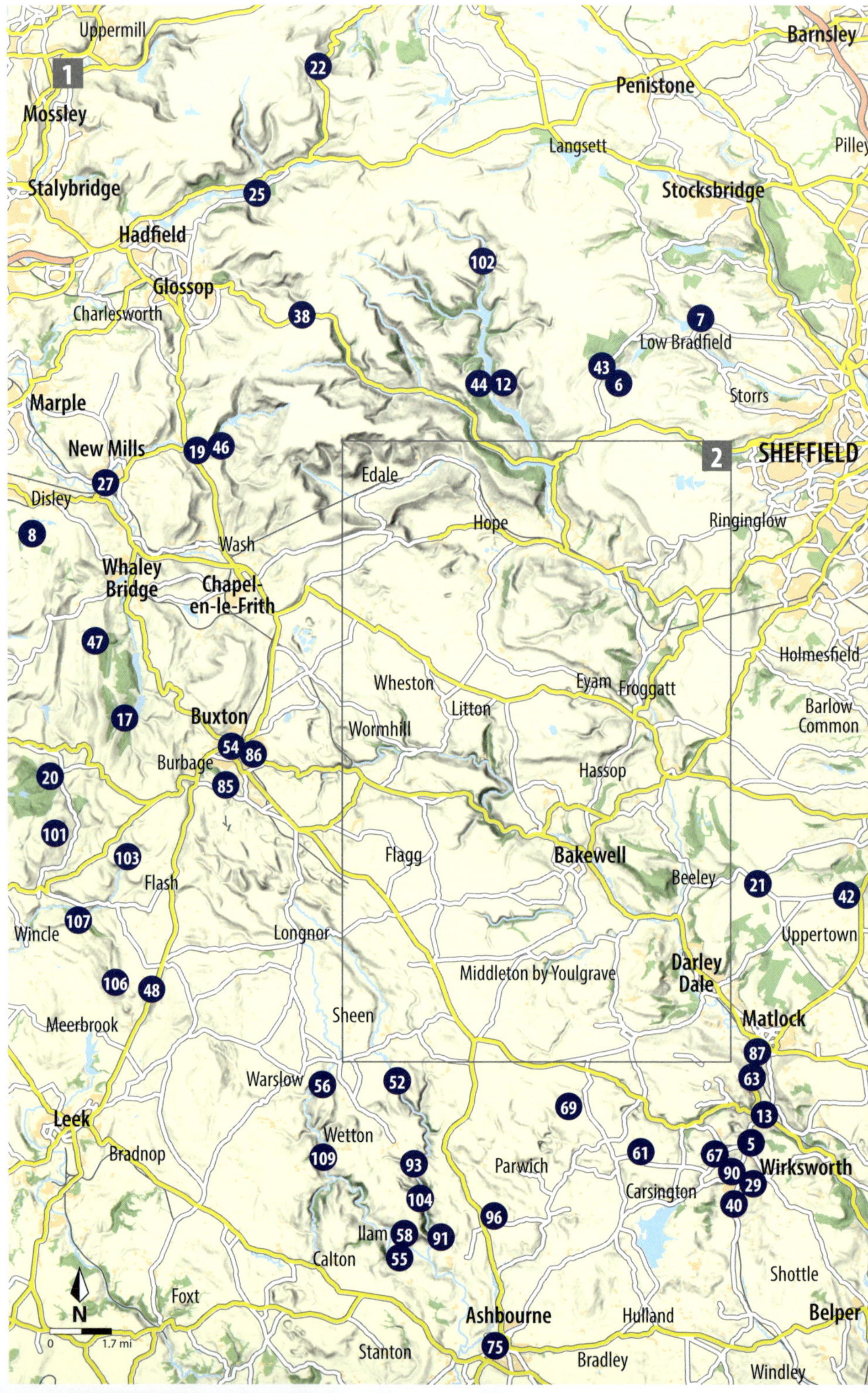

Uppermill
1
22
Barnsley
Mossley
Penistone
Langsett
Pilley
Stalybridge
25
Stocksbridge
Hadfield
102
Glossop
Charlesworth
38
7
Low Bradfield
43
6
44
12
Storrs
Marple
New Mills
19
46
2
SHEFFIELD
27
Edale
Disley
8
Hope
Ringinglow
Wash
Whaley Bridge
Chapel-en-le-Frith
47
Holmesfield
Wheston
Eyam
Froggatt
Barlow Common
17
Litton
Buxton
Wormhill
54
86
Burbage
Hassop
20
85
101
Flagg
Bakewell
103
Beeley
21
42
Flash
107
Wincle
Longnor
Uppertown
Middleton by Youlgrave
Darley Dale
106
48
Meerbrook
Sheen
Matlock
87
Warslow
56
52
63
69
Leek
13
Wetton
5
Bradnop
109
93
Parwich
61
67
Wirksworth
90
29
Carsington
104
40
96
Ilam
58
91
Calton
55
Shottle
Foxt
N
Ashbourne
Hulland
Belper
0
1.7 mi
75
Stanton
Bradley
Windley

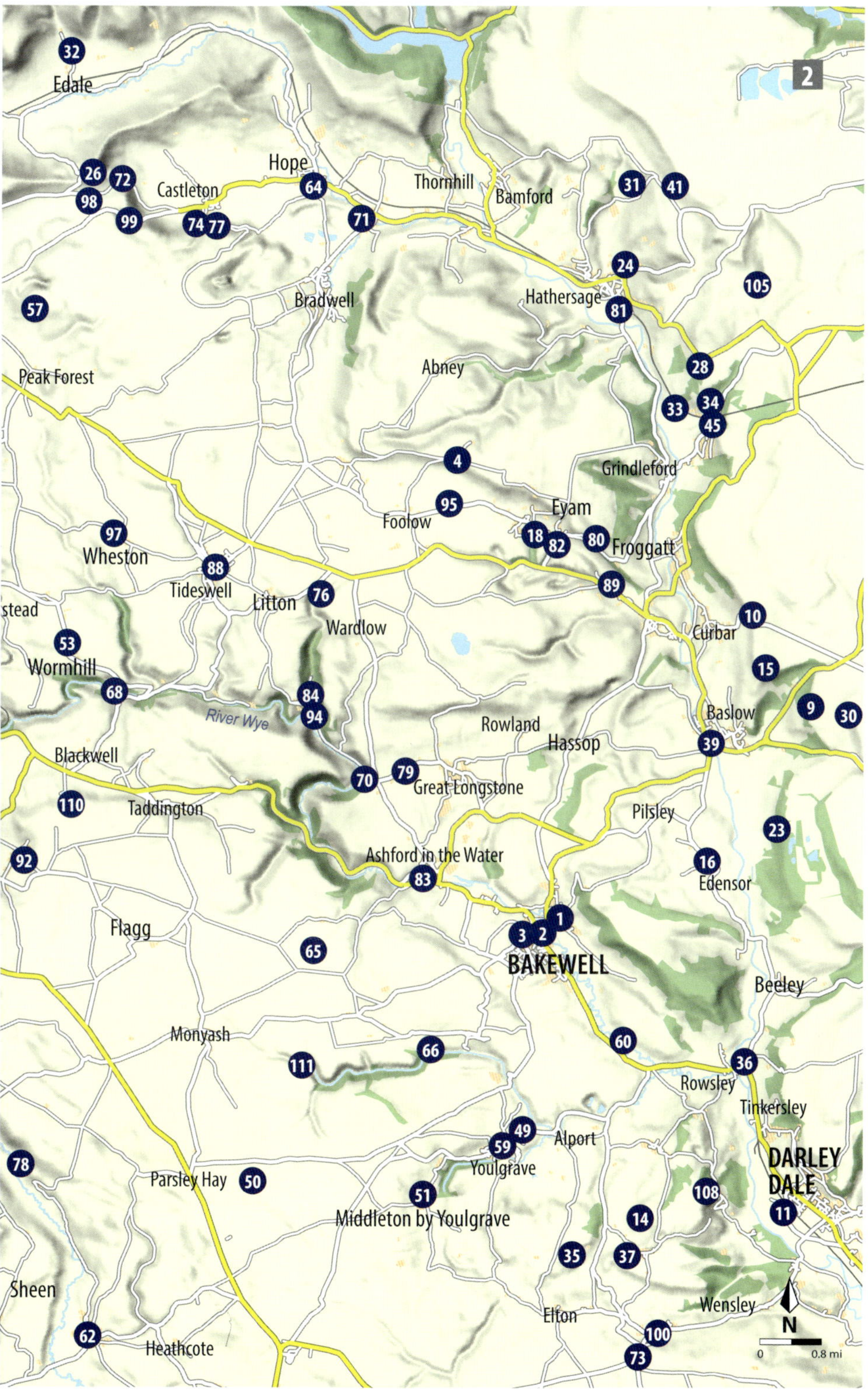
2
Edale
Hope
Castleton
Thornhill
Bamford
Bradwell
Hathersage
Peak Forest
Abney
Grindleford
Eyam
Foolow
Froggatt
Wheston
Tideswell
Litton
stead
Wardlow
Curbar
Wormhill
River Wye
Rowland
Baslow
Hassop
Blackwell
Great Longstone
Taddington
Pilsley
Ashford in the Water
Edensor
Flagg
BAKEWELL
Beeley
Monyash
Rowsley
Tinkersley
Alport
Youlgrave
DARLEY DALE
Parsley Hay
Middleton by Youlgrave
Sheen
Wensley
Elton
Heathcote
N
0
0.8 mi

Michael Glover,
Richard Anderson
111 Places in Sheffield
That You Shouldn't Miss
ISBN 978-3-7408-2348-1

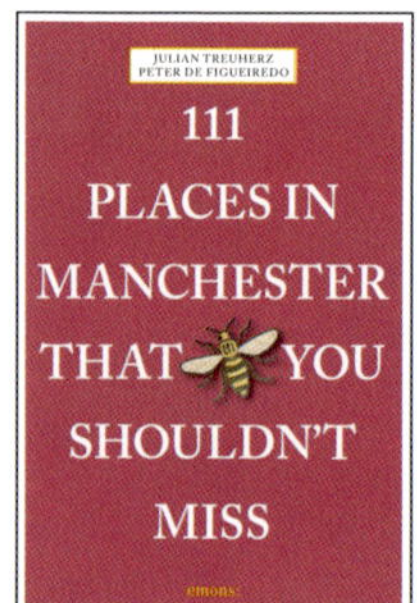

Julian Treuherz,
Peter de Figueiredo
111 Places in Manchester
That You Shouldn't Miss
ISBN 978-3-7408-2645-1

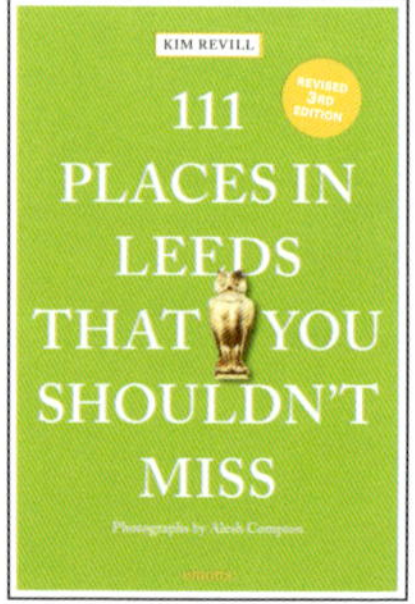

Kim Revill, Alesh Compton
111 Places in Leeds
That You Shouldn't Miss
ISBN 978-3-7408-2059-6

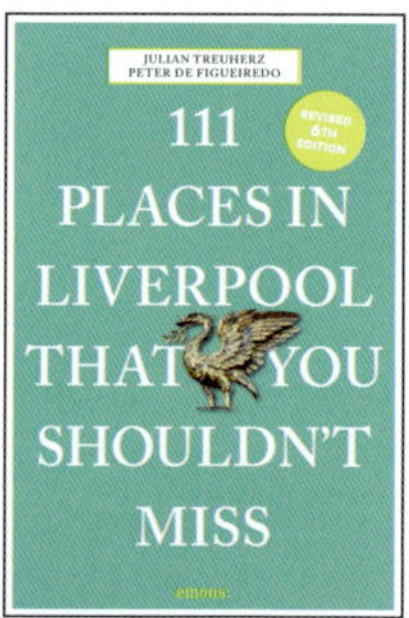

Julian Treuherz,
Peter de Figueiredo
111 Places in Liverpool
That You Shouldn't Miss
ISBN 978-3-7408-2515-7

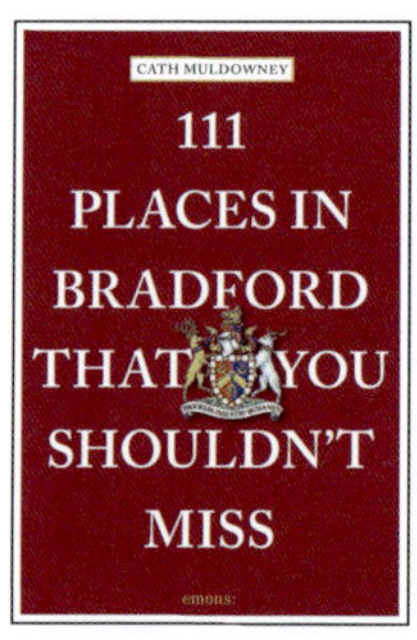

Cath Muldowney
111 Places in Bradford
That You Shouldn't Miss
ISBN 978-3-7408-1427-4

Phil Lee, Rachel Ghent
111 Places in Derby
That You Shouldn't Miss
ISBN 978-3-7408-2432-7

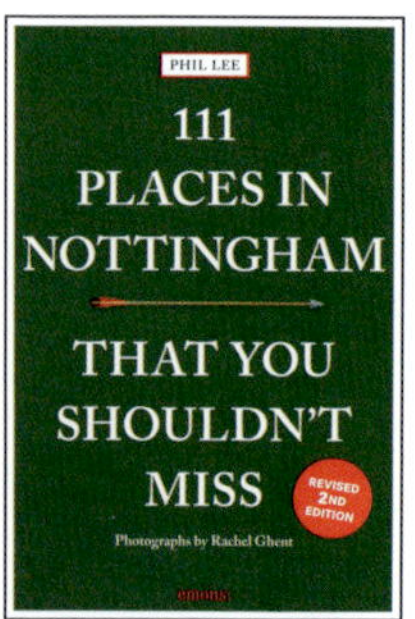

Phil Lee, Rachel Ghent
111 Places in Nottingham
That You Shouldn't Miss
ISBN 978-3-7408-2925-4

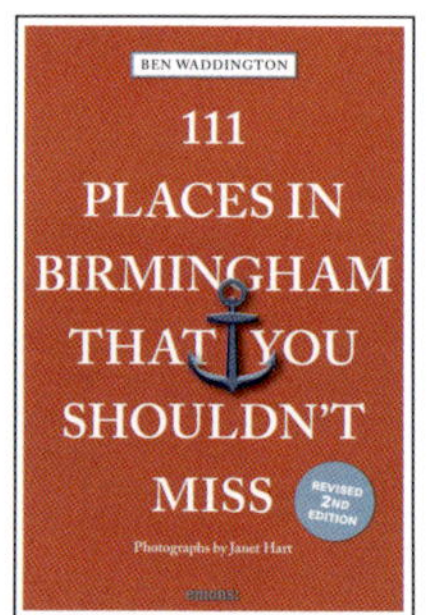

Ben Waddington, Janet Hart
111 Places in Birmingham
That You Shouldn't Miss
ISBN 978-3-7408-2268-2

Solange Berchemin
111 Places in the Lake District
That You Shouldn't Miss
ISBN 978-3-7408-2824-0

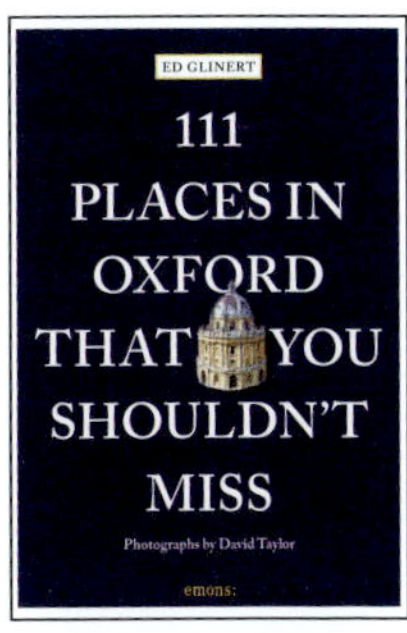

Ed Glinert, David Taylor
111 Places in Oxford That You Shouldn't Miss
ISBN 978-3-7408-1990-3

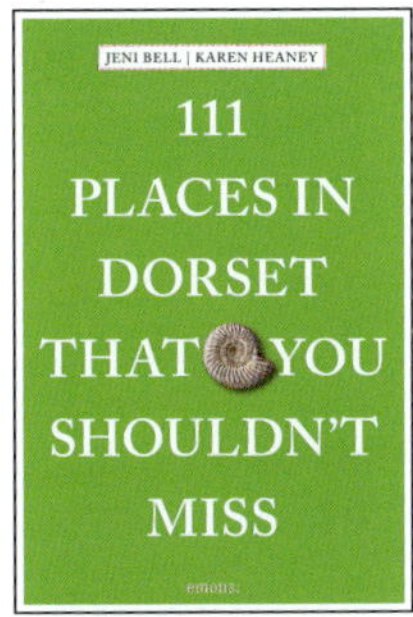

Karen Heaney, Jeni Bell
111 Places in Dorset That You Shouldn't Miss
ISBN 978-3-7408-2146-3

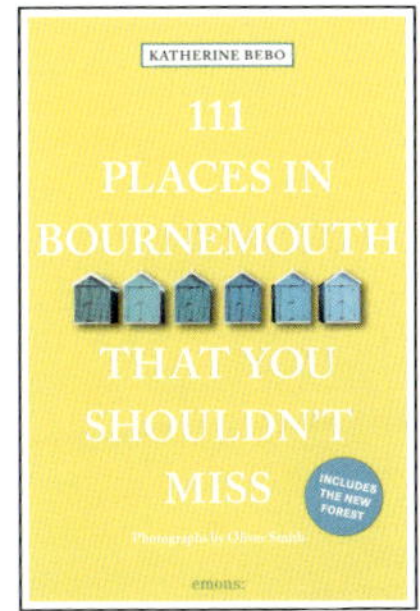

Katherine Bebo, Oliver Smith
111 Places in Bournemouth That You Shouldn't Miss
ISBN 978-3-7408-2646-8

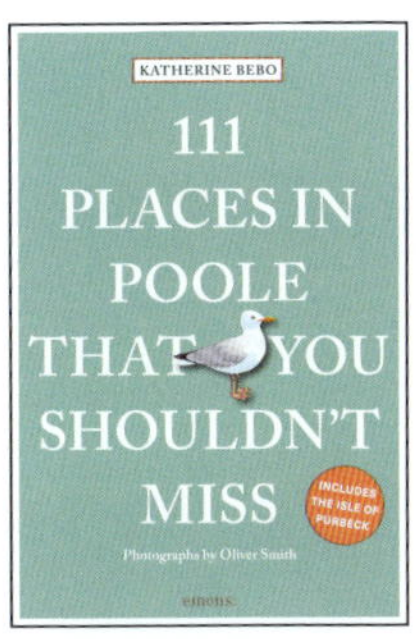

Katherine Bebo, Oliver Smith
111 Places in Poole That You Shouldn't Miss
ISBN 978-3-7408-0598-2

Alexandra Loske
111 Places in Brighton and Lewes That You Shouldn't Miss
ISBN 978-3-7408-1727-5

Norman Miller
111 Places in Hastings & Rye That You Shouldn't Miss
ISBN 978-3-7408-2569-0

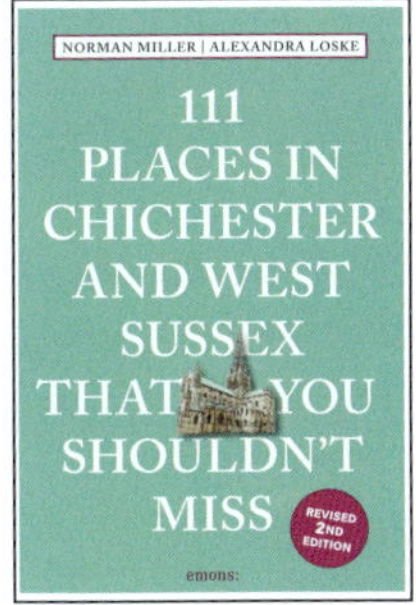

Norman Miller, Alexandra Loske
111 Places in Chichester and West Sussex That You Shouldn't Miss
ISBN 978-3-7408-2807-3

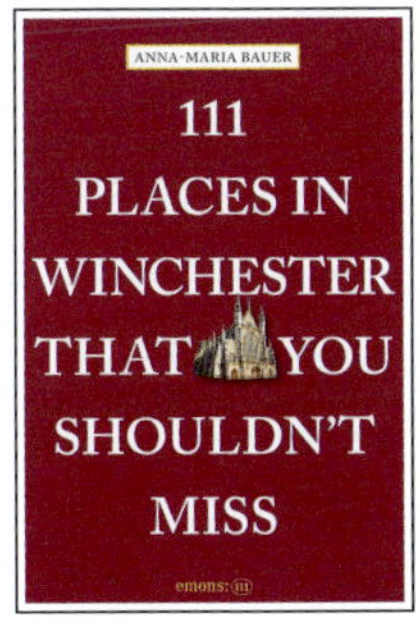

Anna-Maria Bauer
111 Places in Winchester That You Shouldn't Miss
ISBN 978-3-7408-2562-1

Catriona Neil, Adrian Spalding
111 Places in Cornwall That You Shouldn't Miss
ISBN 978-3-7408-2805-9

Martin Booth,
Barbara Evripidou
111 Places in Bristol
That You Shouldn't Miss
ISBN 978-3-7408-2512-6

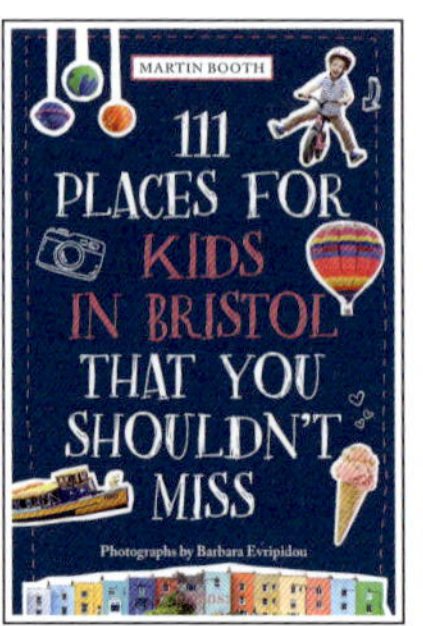

Martin Booth, Barbara Evripidou
111 Places for Kids in Bristol
That You Shouldn't Miss
ISBN 978-3-7408-1665-0

David Taylor
111 Places in Northumberland
That You Shouldn't Miss
ISBN 978-3-7408-2923-0

Ed Glinert, David Taylor
111 Places in Yorkshire
That You Shouldn't Miss
ISBN 978-3-7408-1167-9

Ed Glinert, Karin Tearle
111 Places in Essex
That You Shouldn't Miss
ISBN 978-3-7408-1593-6

John Sykes, Birgit Weber
111 Places in London
That You Shouldn't Miss
ISBN 978-3-7408-2928-5

Alicia Edwards
111 Places for Kids in London
That You Shouldn't Miss
ISBN 978-3-7408-2196-8

Michael Glover, Benedict Flett
111 Hidden Art Treasures
in London That You
Shouldn't Miss
ISBN 978-3-7408-1576-9

Terry Philpot, Karin Tearle
111 Literary Places in London
That You Shouldn't Miss
ISBN 978-3-7408-1954-5

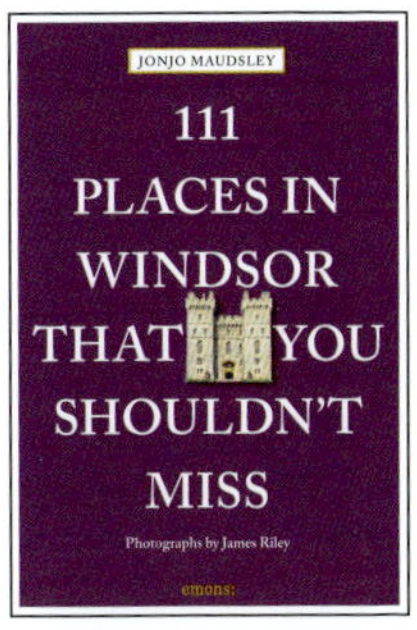

Jonjo Maudsley, James Riley
111 Places in Windsor That You Shouldn't Miss
ISBN 978-3-7408-2009-1

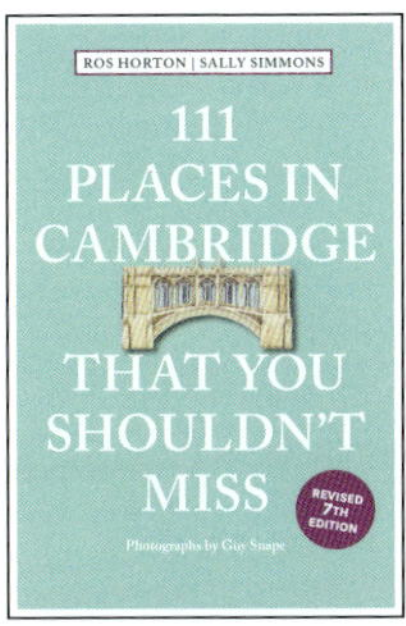

Rosalind Horton, Sally Simmons, Guy Snape
111 Places in Cambridge That You Shouldn't Miss
ISBN 978-3-7408-2376-4

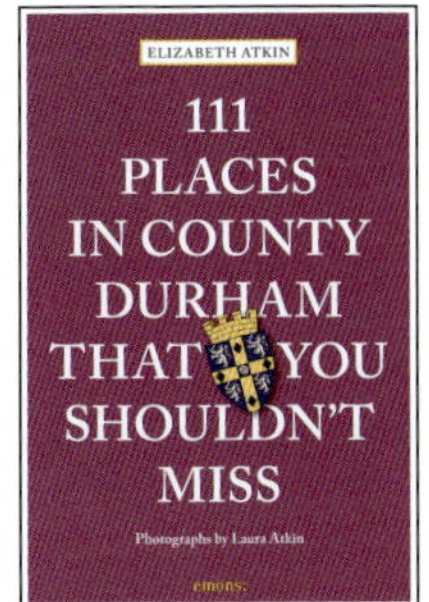

Elizabeth Atkin, Laura Atkin
111 Places in County Durham That You Shouldn't Miss
ISBN 978-3-7408-1426-7

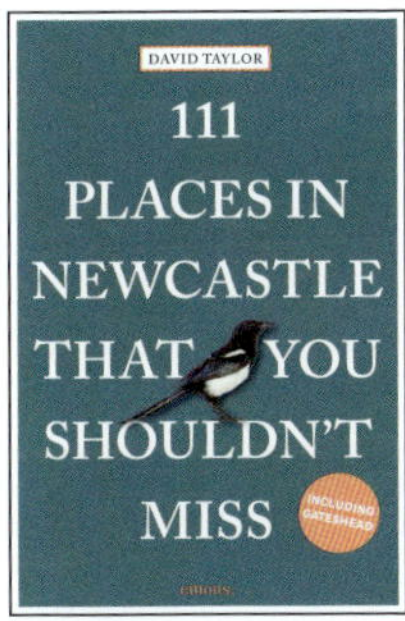

David Taylor
111 Places in Newcastle That You Shouldn't Miss
ISBN 978-3-7408-1043-6

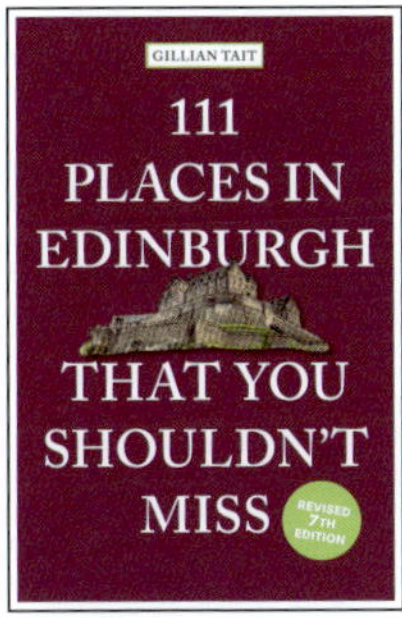

Gillian Tait
111 Places in Edinburgh That You Shouldn't Miss
ISBN 978-3-7408-2575-1

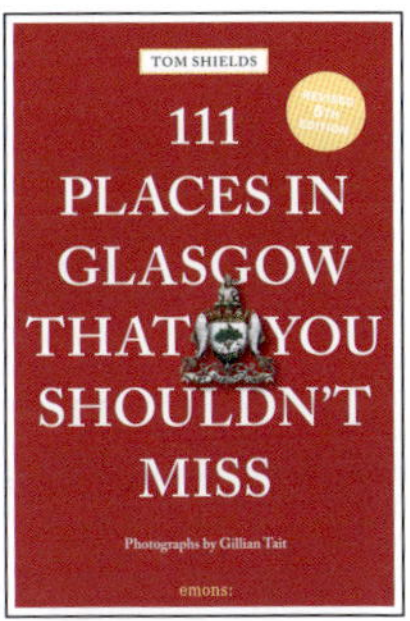

Tom Shields, Gillian Tait
111 Places in Glasgow That You Shouldn't Miss
ISBN 978-3-7408-2922-3

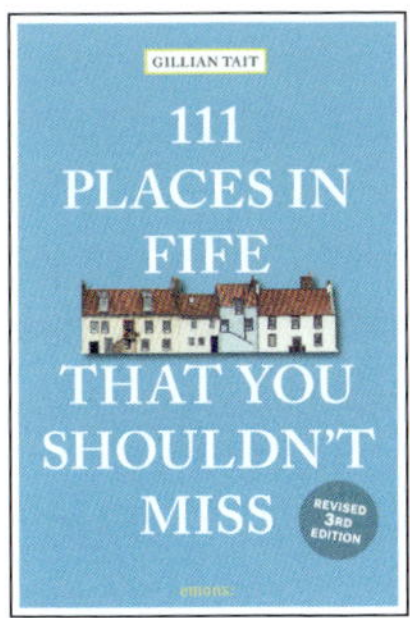

Gillian Tait
111 Places in Fife That You Shouldn't Miss
ISBN 978-3-7408-2806-6

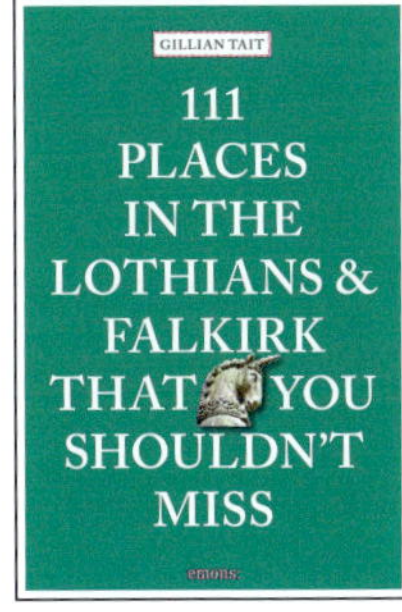

Gillian Tait
111 Places in the Lothians and Falkirk That You Shouldn't Miss
ISBN 978-3-7408-1569-1

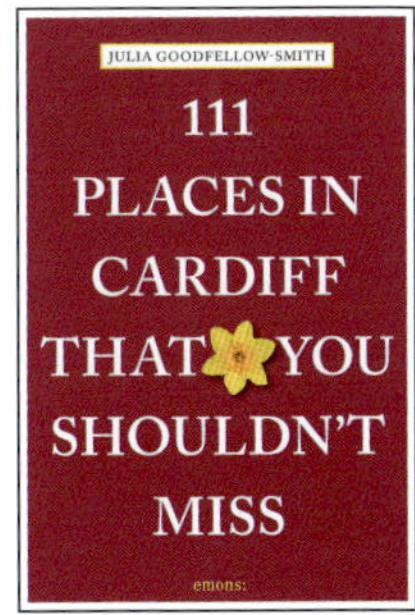

Julia Goodfellow-Smith
111 Places in Cardiff That You Shouldn't Miss
ISBN 978-3-7408-2465-5

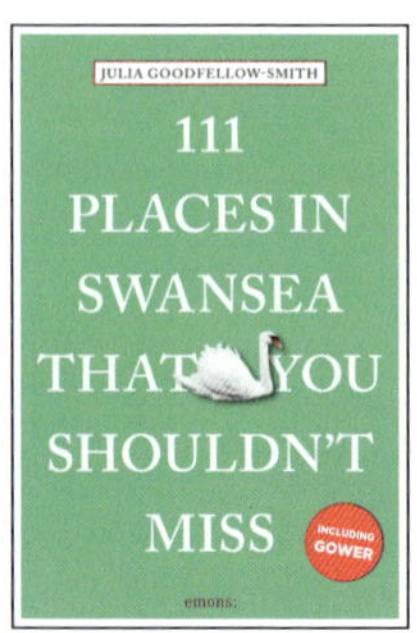

Julia Goodfellow-Smith
111 Places in Swansea That You Shouldn't Miss
ISBN 978-3-7408-2065-7

Jo-Anne Elikann, Susan Lusk
111 Places in New York That You Must Not Miss
ISBN 978-3-7408-2400-6

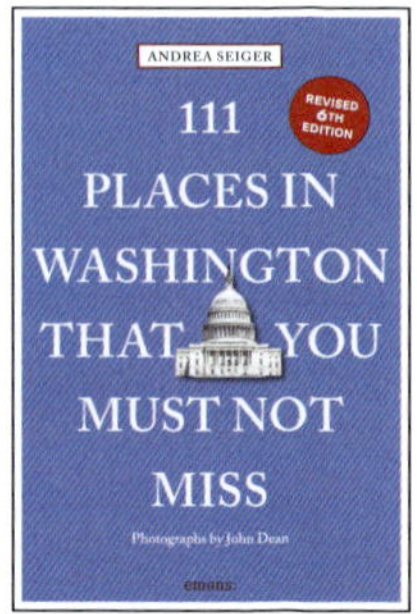

Andrea Seiger, John Dean
111 Places in Washington That You Must Not Miss
ISBN 978-3-7408-2656-7

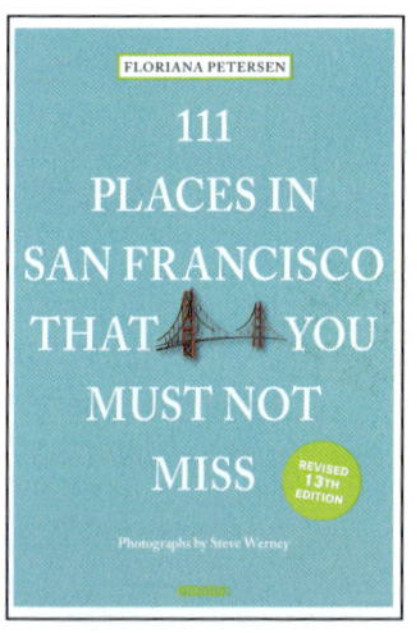

Floriana Petersen, Steve Werney
111 Places in San Francisco That You Must Not Miss
ISBN 978-3-7408-2882-0

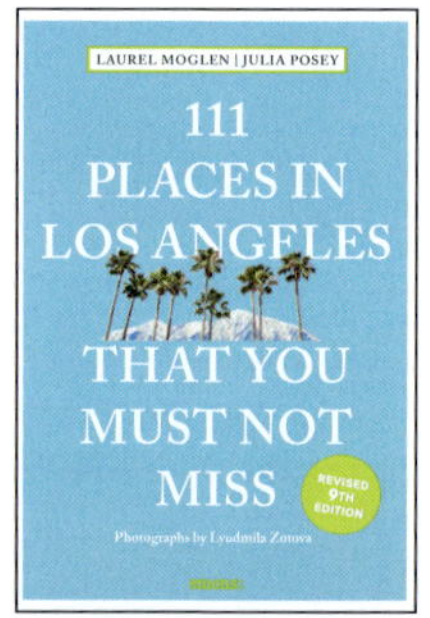

Laurel Moglen, Julia Posey, Lyudmila Zotova
111 Places in Los Angeles That You Must Not Miss
ISBN 978-3-7408-2573-7

Amy Bizzarri, Susie Inverso
111 Places in Chicago That You Must Not Miss
ISBN 978-3-7408-2402-0

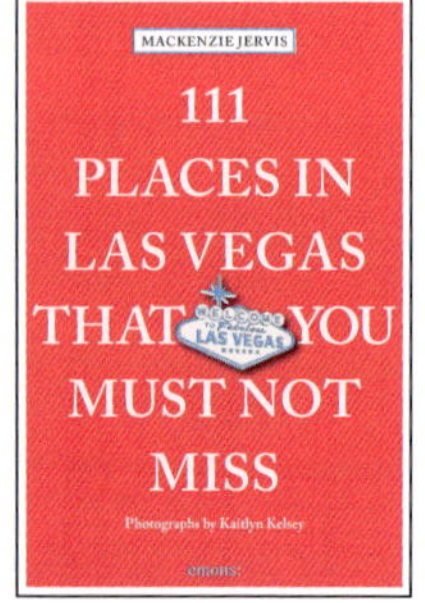

Mackenzie Jervis, Kaitlyn Kelsey
111 Places in Las Vegas That You Must Not Miss
ISBN 978-3-7408-2467-9

Gordon Streisand, Alexandra Streisand
111 Places in Miami and the Keys That You Must Not Miss
ISBN 978-3-7408-2403-7

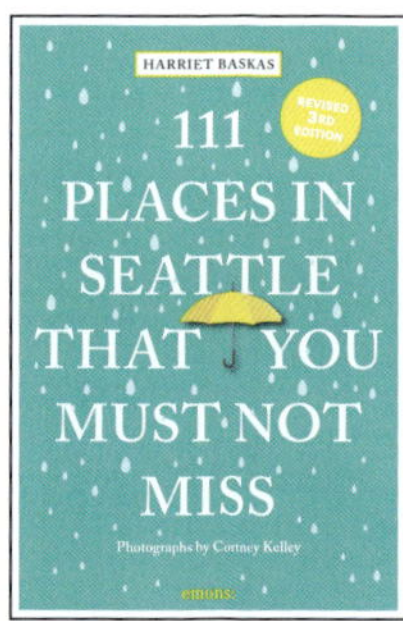

Harriet Baskas, Cortney Kelley
111 Places in Seattle That You Must Not Miss
ISBN 978-3-7408-2375-7

Acknowledgements

First and foremost, I must thank Laura Olk at Emons, for readily recognising the need for a Peak District volume in the *111 Places* series. And then warmest thanks to my genial editor, Tania Taylor, for gamely trying to keep my unchecked enthusiasm for the Peak in check.

My good friend and ace photographer Chris Gilbert's knowledge of the Peak District is encyclopaedic, and we worked together as a team to come up with many of the places that appear here. So thank you Chris, for your sterling work on this, our second book together.

Then I must express my gratitude to two groups of people who, perhaps more than any others, introduced me to many of these 'unmissable' places, which I wouldn't have known about but for them. Firstly, members of the now sadly diminished Ranger Service of the Peak District National Park. Rangers were the eyes and ears of the National Park, and when I first moved here over 50 years ago, I spent many a happy day out walking with them, getting to know the land and its stories from the people who knew them best. Many have since passed on, but thank you all for your kindness, your patience and your expert shared knowledge.

The second group is known as the Escape Committee, a walking group formed mostly by early retirees from the National Park authority who meet up once a month for a walk, ending up at a pub for lunch. They've taken me to places I never knew in the Peak and far beyond – to countries as far away as Iceland and Jordan – so my warm thanks to all of them too.

Finally, as ever, I must express my deeply felt love and gratitude to my wife Val, who has once again put up with me slaving over a hot keyboard when I should probably have been mowing the lawn or decorating the back bedroom. As am I, this book is dedicated to her, to our three wonderful children, Claire, Neil and Iain, and to our three beautiful granddaughters, Amy, Chloe and Holly.

Roly Smith was known as 'Mr Peak District' when he was Head of Information Services for the Peak District National Park. The author of over 90 books on the Peak District and Britain, he was recently described as one of Britain's most respected and knowledgeable countryside writers.

Chris Gilbert is a professional photographer, photography teacher and illustrator. He lives in the small village of Cressbrook in the middle of the Peak District National Park in the UK. He bought his first SLR camera with his first pay cheque in 1981 and has been taking photographs ever since. His work features regularly in local magazines and publications and he has been working closely with the Peak District National Park Authority since 2014 to promote the area's qualities and help visitors.